The Manhattan Diaries Series

Behind the Velvet Rope
NYC's Grooming Secrets Revealed

Manhattan Allure
Just Like That

The Manhattan Diaries Series

Manhattan Allure – Just Like That

Manhattan Vitality – Just Like That

Manhattan Lifestyle – Just Like That

Manhattan Ambition – Just Like That

The Manhattan Diaries Series

Behind the Velvet Rope
NYC's Grooming
Secrets Revealed

Manhattan Allure
Just Like That

PAIGE MC CLINTE

Urban Chronicles Publishing House
an imprint of The Ridge Publishing Group
Coeur d'Alene, Idaho, U.S.A.

DISCLAIMER: The ideas, concepts, and opinions expressed in The Manhattan Diaries Series (hereinafter referred to as "Series") are intended to help readers make thoughtful and informed decisions about their lifestyle. This Series is sold with the understanding that author and publisher are not rendering medical advice of any kind, nor is this Series intended to replace the medical advice, nor to diagnose, prescribe, or treat any disease, condition, illness, or injury. It should not be used as a substitute for treatment by or the advice of a professional healthcare provider. It is recommended that before beginning any diet or exercise program, including any aspect of the Series, you receive full medical clearance from a licensed healthcare provider. Although the author and publisher have endeavored to ensure that the information provided in the Series is complete and accurate, the author and publisher claim no responsibility to any person or entity for any liability, loss, or damage caused or alleged to be caused directly or indirectly as a result of the use, application, or interpretation of the material in this Series, or any errors or omissions in the Series.

CREDIT: This book was written with limited assistance of ChatGPT, an AI language model developed by OpenAI. The collaboration provided unique insights and support in crafting content. The book cover was created using Midjourney tools and Adobe Photoshop, ensuring a visually captivating design.

Library of Congress Control Number: 2024917266

Behind the Velvet Rope: NYC's Grooming Secrets Revealed by Paige McClinte

ISBN: 978-1-956905-14-4 (e-book)
ISBN: 978-1-956905-13-7 (Softcover)

1. Health & Fitness / Beauty & Grooming. 2. Self-Help / Personal Growth / General. 3. Body, Mind & Spirit / Inspirational & Personal Growth. I. Title. II. Series.

First Edition: August 2024

Printed in the United States of America

Contents

The Manhattan Diaries Series

DARE TO REIMAGINE YOURSELF . . .

21 Steps to Reinvent and Discover a Side of You Manhattan's Never Seen

The Manhattan Diaries Series presents:

Manhattan Allure—Just Like That mini-series (books 1–5)

Manhattan Vitality—Just Like That mini-series (books 6–10)

Manhattan Lifestyle—Just Like That mini-series (books 11–16)

Manhattan Ambition—Just Like That mini-series (books 17–21)

Meet the Author

https://www.LAMoeszinger.com

Meet the Publisher, Urban Chronicles Publishing House

https://www.NewYouniversityChronicles.com

Step into the whirlwind world of New York's glitzy underbelly, where the scintillating secrets and laugh-out-loud confessions of a metropolitan woman are laid bare by someone truly in the know. Through essays pulled from her chic "Manhattanite's Survival Guide—Success in the City," L invites us on an unforgettable strut from her glamorous youth, through her middle-aged mazes, and into her fabulous sixties.

For the juiciest tidbits about L's life, her "Manhattan Chronicles" blog is the place to be. This blog is an unfiltered dive into L's world, from her spiritual musings to her meticulous weigh-ins to her New Youniversity Chronicles—The Manhattan Diaries series—personal tales. Dive into her cosmos at her blog site: https://www.ManhattanChronicles.com.

The Manhattan Diaries Series

Behind the Velvet Rope
NYC's Grooming
Secrets Revealed

Manhattan Allure
Just Like That

Introduction: Champagne, Secrets, and Stilettos – The Enchanted Beauty Chronicles of New York City!

Hey there, urban explorers! When you step out into the dazzling lights of the city that never sleeps, do you ever wonder about the secrets hidden behind the velvet rope of glamour and style? Do you stride through the bustling streets with the confidence of a true New Yorker, or are you still on the path to discovering the city's best-kept grooming secrets? Let me tell you, darlings, the glitter of your future should always outshine the sparkle of your past, and I've got more than just a glimpse to offer. Welcome to "Behind the Velvet Rope: NYC's Grooming Secrets Revealed."

In this enchanting journey, I'm going to take you behind the scenes of the city's grooming elite. Success in New York City isn't just about wit or navigating the chic streets—it's about making an unforgettable impression at every swanky event, from uptown soirees to downtown happenings. I've rubbed shoulders with the glitterati, sipped cocktails at the trendiest spots, and uncovered the grooming secrets that keep NYC's finest looking their best. But remember, true charm starts from within.

Consider this your VIP ticket to a luxury, limited edition of The Manhattan Diaries series, experience. Whether you dive in over leisurely days, savor it week by week, or sip cocktails on Manhattan rooftops while flipping through the pages, the pace is entirely yours. Picture yourself delving into a chapter with your morning latte or conquering the entire book during a weekend getaway. Within these pages, you'll discover the keys to unlocking a new, refined version of yourself, and the magnetism that follows will leave you astounded.

BEHIND THE VELVET ROPE

As we journey through these pages together, I'll be your confidante, revealing how easily you can conquer the concrete jungle. This guide isn't just about grooming tips; it's a rebirth of your spirit, your relationships, and your aspirations in the city. Join me in uncovering the secrets that will make you shine as brightly as the city skyline. I'm not just committed to helping you rise among the city's elite; I'm here to ignite the fire in your heart that propels you to your most spectacular self. Embrace it and the energy of New York will be yours to command!

My passion for this city-centric guide stems from my own personal journey, full of highs and lows, passion and heartbreaks. Like many city dwellers, I had to forge my own path, sometimes veering off the beaten track. But today, I stand here, ready to inspire you to conquer your city, too, cocktail in hand.

As time sails on the Hudson River, our diverse life paths eventually intersect. For me, the whirlwind of career pursuits, downtown soirees, and self-discovery converged with my love for the city leading me to work with the Urban Chronicles Publishing House.

New York City isn't exclusive to celebrities or trust fund beneficiaries; it's yours too, whether you're in your chic twenties or your sophisticated sixties. Embrace this journey with me as we embark on a path to city stardom in this second step—The Manhattan Diaries series is a twenty-one step journey; twenty-one books to reinvent and discover a side of you Manhattan's never met.

"Behind the Velvet Rope" equips you with the tools to not only dream big but to seize those dreams. I'm here as your city guardian, ensuring you realize that everything you crave starts within. Indulge in the city's finest, and watch as your dream job, penthouse, or perfect partner follows suit. If you've got city-sized dreams, this series is your golden key! I've seen friends rise to city stardom time and time again, providing that as you align within, the city will reflect it back in glitz and glamour. That's a promise straight from the heart of New York.

Relying on The Manhattan Diaries series it has always been my go-to source. Whenever the city threw a curveball my way, this series navigated me right back to my radiant path. The allure of always being on top keeps me returning to these pages, and trust me, it's far more exhilarating than settling for mediocrity.

With each page you turn, you'll discover the blueprint, insider secrets, and the support you need to make your city journey a thrilling adventure. This series is tailored for everyone, from the ambitious career seekers to the social butterflies and empire builders.

There are countless ways to rise in the Big Apple, but if you're searching for the chicest route, it's right here in The Manhattan Diaries. Immerse yourself in its delights while reciting positive mantras, and let the city's vibrancy chase away any doubts; and, in this case, allowing your city star to shine. To truly reign, sometimes we need to shed our old sequins and embrace our radiant selves.

Navigating the Metropolis with The Manhattan Diaries

Welcome to "Behind the Velvet Rope: NYC's Grooming Secrets Revealed." Think of this edition of The Manhattan Diaries as your very own cosmopolitan diary, as interactive as an invitation to Manhattan's most exclusive soirees. Each chapter is enriched with journal pages, waiting for your Manhattan musings and anecdotes. Whether you want to record the day's chic highlights in your city beats or delve into deep reflections in your city confessions, these pages are yours to fill; also see Cocktails and Chronicles: "Journal Pages: Pen Your Tales" at the end of the book to record even more details.

But . . .

1 Before you start jotting down your thoughts, take a moment to breathe. Close your eyes, and in that quiet moment, whisper a heartfelt "thank you" to the city that never sleeps. Feel that rush of gratitude, as if you've just scored front row tickets to New York Fashion Week. Let that "thank you" resonate deep within your heart—because that, my friends, is the magic of Manhattan.

2 Begin by detailing the fabulous strides you've made since reading the last glamorous advice. Write them down under "Your Triumphs," and bask in the Fifth Avenue feeling that washes over you.

3 Once you've celebrated your triumphs, turn the page to "Your Goals" and script your aspirations. Reflect on what's left to conquer in your metropolitan journey, capturing your next steps in this transformational saga.

Throughout The Manhattan Diaries series, you'll find timeless "inspirational quotes" that are as iconic as the Empire State Building itself. Think of them as your cosmopolitan compass, guiding your city journey. Relish them like sips from a crystal glass at a swanky Manhattan penthouse party, and let them resonate deep within your urban soul.

As you approach the end of each guide, you'll discover a "City Roundup." Here, you'll find a chic recap summarizing all the insider tips from your city escapade, ensuring you never miss a New York beauty minute.

So, get ready to peel back the curtain on NYC's best-kept grooming secrets, darlings. Behind the velvet rope awaits a world of glamour, style, and endless possibilities. It's time to shine brighter than the city lights.

CHAMPAGNE, SECRETS, AND STILETTOS

Behind the Velvet Rope: NYC's Grooming Secrets Revealed

Dive into the next edition, sweethearts—the sparkling sequel in our addictive Manhattan escapade: "Behind the Velvet Rope: NYC's Grooming Secrets Revealed."

Ah, New York! A city where secrets shimmer as brightly as the skyline, and where behind every red velvet rope lies a tale of allure waiting to be unveiled. Picture this: a hidden penthouse in SoHo, golden elevators, crystal chandeliers, and just beyond those hushed doors? Manhattan's finest, looking every bit the part.

In this enthralling addition to The Manhattan Diaries, you'll be whisked away to the clandestine corners of the city—where A-listers, moguls, and fashionistas transform into radiant urban legends. But hold on, it's not just about the latest mascara or the most intoxicating perfume. Oh no, it's about those whispered rituals, the guarded secrets, and the allure only New York can bottle.

But remember, it's not just about the glitz. No, it's about the soul behind the sparkle. The audacious spirit, the tales hidden beneath every expertly applied smoky eye, and the passion that fuels every New Yorker's glow.

Join me, darling, as we waltz into the heart of the city's glam universe with "Behind the Velvet Rope." Because in Manhattan, beauty isn't just skin deep—it's the beat of the city's heart. So, pop the bubbly, put on that bewitching shade of lipstick, and let's delve into the city's most coveted beauty mysteries. The night awaits, and in NYC, we don't just shine—we dazzle.

BEHIND THE VELVET ROPE

Meet the Maestros Behind the Curtain

Welcome to the glittering realm of The Manhattan Diaries series, penned by an eclectic group of scribes who know how to make words shimmer just like that Midtown skyline. Each of these writers possesses the kind of Manhattan moxie that's as electrifying as a Saturday night at Studio 54. Picture the literary equivalent of the fabulous foursome from "Sex and the City," but with a little extra Manhattan mascara.

Our authors, darlings, aren't just writers; they're connoisseurs of all things NYC, dishing out stories with the precision of a Fifth Avenue stylist crafting the perfect blowout. Their tales are imbued with the kind of insider knowledge only those who've sipped martinis at the city's most secretive spots can truly understand.

So, as you delve into the pages of The Manhattan Diaries know that you're not just reading words, you're sipping on the prose of New York's finest literary mixologists. Here's to a journey as sparkling and unforgettable as a New York night out. Cheers, darling!

Behind the Scenes with the Urban Chronicles Publishing House

In the whirlwind of New York's high society, the Urban Chronicles Publishing House has emerged as the ultimate style sage for modern-day self-help. Over a cosmopolitan-fueled decade, they've become the city's go-to curators for crafting that sought-after, enviable life. The Manhattan Diaries? Envision it as your exclusive, VIP backstage pass, dripping with Upper East Side allure.

If you've ever pictured yourself sashaying through Manhattan with poise, if you've craved that skyline backdrop to your impeccable life, or if you simply seek the secrets whispered in the plush corners of the city's most exclusive clubs—The Manhattan Diaries is your ticket. Crafted under the elite banner, Urban Chronicles Publishing House, this imprint doesn't just offer you insights; it's your personal invite to the city's most glamorous circles.

> **Forever en Vogue**. Everyone, from the Wall Street moguls to the aspiring Broadway stars, dreams of basking in New York's radiant glow of living a life drenched in style and substance. The wisdom in The Manhattan Diaries is as timeless as a Fifth Avenue romance, ensuring you're always en vogue.

> **A Blueprint for the Elite**. Nestled within these pages are the golden rules of city living, from mastering the cocktail chatter to undergoing a dazzling reinvention. Whether you're a seasoned socialite, an ambitious parent, or a fresh-eyed dreamer, these guides have something to make your heart race a little faster.

> **The Perfect Accessory**. Their petite stature makes these guides a seamless fit for your Prada clutch or your gym tote. Think of them as your urban survival kit—a blend of wisdom and wit that's as crucial as your red lipstick for those Manhattan nights.

Take a sip of this rich concoction, and let the Urban Chronicles Publishing House unlock Manhattan, unveiling a New York you only dreamed of. Welcome to the allure of the elite, darling.

Unveiling The Ridge Publishing Group

Picture The Ridge Publishing Group as the rising star on New York's literary and entertainment horizon. Envision an eclectic empire—books, cinema, and board games—setting the stage to become the world's haute couture of theological discourse. Think Fifth Avenue for theological resources: luxurious, elite, and unparalleled.

Dive into their esteemed collections. They hold the keys to the illustrious Guardians of Biblical Truth Publishing Group and the evocative New Narrated Study Bible (NNSB) series. Delve deeper and find the Hoyle

Theology Publishing Group and its opulent Hoyle Theology Encyclopedia—a treasure trove for the cerebral sophisticate. And for those who like their theology paired with a cinematic flair, there's the Documentaries in Print Publishing Group with its tantalizing series like Defending the Faith. And, of course, for those cocktail nights with a side of divine strategy, the Heaven's Seminary board games and card decks offer a chic twist.

But that's not all. The Ridge Publishing Group is more than a theological publishing powerhouse; it's a brand. Alongside its flagship, it flaunts trendy imprints: AuthorsDoor Group and AuthorsDoor Leadership (check them out at the glamorous digital boulevard of https://www.AuthorsDoor.com), the ritzy Urban Chronicles Publishing House and New Youniversity Chronicles (make your reservation at https://www.LAMoeszinger.com), and the novel delights of Ethan Fox Books (sip your martini and browse https://www.EthanFox Books.com).

For a sneak peek into the world where theology meets Manhattan glamour, rendezvous at their digital penthouse: https://www.Ridge PublishingGroup.com. It's theology made chic.

A NOTE TO THE READER

Typos in this book? Errors (and inconsistencies) can get through proofreaders, so if you do find any typos or grammatical errors in this book, I'd be very grateful if you could let me know using this email address typos@LAMoeszinger.com. Thank you ☺

1

Sky-High Lashes and City Lights: Mascara Secrets of the Metropolis

Manhattan, a city where the glow isn't only from the skyline—it's reflected in the eyes of its dreamers, as their lashes fan out tales of aspiration, passion, and a hint of mischief. In this metropolis of continuous shimmer, it's not just about capturing a glance; it's about holding it—with drama, depth, and a dash of dazzle.

Now imagine: You're dancing down Madison Avenue, and while the world may be enchanted by the swing of your hips or the sway of your dress, it's truly the allure of your eyes, framed by those sky-high lashes, that have them spellbound. That, my darling, is the Manhattan Blink of Fame—a subtle art that speaks not just of beauty, but of stories untold and promises unspoken.

In this captivating chapter of The Manhattan Diaries, we'll unravel the mystique behind those mesmerizing lashes. From the soft, feather-like flutter that whispers sweet secrets to the bold, audacious sweep that declares the world is yours for the taking, you'll learn the craft of captivating with just a bat of an eye.

But this isn't just about aesthetics—no. It's about harnessing the city's essence, ensuring that with every upward glance towards the skyline or every sultry stare across a crowded room, you echo Manhattan's pulsating heart. It's about ensuring that your eyes, much like the city's iconic buildings, always reach for the stars.

Join me, as we journey through boutique salons and clandestine beauty parlors, unveiling the secrets of lashes that don't merely flutter but soar. Because, sweetheart, in Manhattan, every blink is a chance for seduction. So, let your lashes kiss the sky and let the city fall at your feet. Welcome to The Manhattan Diaries—where your gaze can hold as much magic as the city's twinkling lights.

The Allure of the Manhattan Blink

In The Allure of the Manhattan Blink, we delve into the captivating world of Manhattan's most enchanting feature—a gaze that tells a thousand stories, all hidden behind the flutter of perfectly sculpted lashes. This isn't just about the physical allure of eye makeup; it's about embracing and reflecting the soul of the city itself, where each blink is a chapter of an untold story, each glance a silent whisper of dreams and desires.

- **The Enigmatic Smile**. As you ready to embrace the city, let your smile be your most mystifying charm. It's a smile that speaks volumes without uttering a word, leaving onlookers intrigued, craving to uncover the tales hidden behind it.

- **The Half-Told Tale**. In your fleeting looks, leave a narrative half-revealed. It's about offering a glimpse into your day's adventures or the night's plans but never revealing the full picture. Your gaze should be a captivating teaser, a fragment of a tale that kindles curiosity and imagination.

- **The Glimpse of a Secret**. As you navigate the city's canvas, let there be a hint of a mystery in your eyes—a depth not fully understood, an emotion not completely deciphered. These subtle, nuanced expressions create an aura of intrigue around you, a riddle that others feel compelled to solve.

- **The Unanswered Question in Your Goodbye**. Make your parting glance an unsolved enigma. Whether it's a playful twinkle that's open to interpretation or a profound look that suggests deeper layers of your persona, leave them pondering, leave them enchanted, leave them longing to understand more.

- **The Whispered Farewell**. Infuse your farewells with a tone of secrecy, as if your eyes are sharing a confidential truth. This whispered goodbye, laden with unspoken tales, suggests a world of hidden stories, leaving those you meet captivated by the mysteries you might behold.

- **The Enigmatic Accessory**. As you traverse through the city, let your eyes be the enigmatic accessory that starts silent conversations. A glance that holds a story, a look that carries a legacy—each expression should be a statement that invites questions and piques curiosity, a symbol of the enigmas that encircle you.

- **The Unfinished Conversation**. Deliberately leave a conversation incomplete in your gaze, a thought hanging in the balance. It could be an emotion you display but don't fully explain, or a sentiment you express but leave tantalizingly open.

- **The Veil of Privacy**. In a world where sharing is commonplace, maintain a veil of mystery in your eyes. Be selective about what they reveal, offering just enough to intrigue but never enough to unveil the full story.

- **The Seductive Glance Back**. As you move through Manhattan, give a final, fleeting look back. It's a glance that says you're part of the city but always a step beyond, a visual promise that there is more to your story. This last look should be seductive and suggestive, a silent assurance that while you may be stepping out of the scene, your story in the tapestry of Manhattan is far from over.

The Allure of the Manhattan Blink, it's not merely about the visual impact, but about the promise of more—more tales, more depth, more facets of your intriguing persona yet to be unveiled. It's about ensuring that your presence in the city isn't just a fleeting moment, but an ellipsis in the grand narrative of Manhattan's ceaseless allure. It's an art form, where each glance is a meticulously crafted act, leaving a trail of mystique that echoes through the city streets, long after your silhouette has merged with the city's skyline.

Your Triumphs: The Manhattan Blink Activities

Inspirational Quote

BE THE CHANGE THAT YOU WISH TO SEE IN THE WORLD. — Mahatma Gandhi

Your Goals: Intentions and Thoughts

Unveiling the Mascara Craft

In Unveiling the Mascara Craft, we step into the glamorous world of Manhattan's beauty, where the simple act of applying mascara is elevated to an art form, a delicate dance of brushes and wands that mirrors the city's own rhythm and flair. This chapter is not just a tutorial on how to apply mascara; it's a journey into the heart of Manhattan's beauty culture, where each stroke of the brush is as meaningful and deliberate as the city's pulsating energy.

➢ **The Magic Wand**. Here, we explore the mascara wand as more than just a beauty tool—it's a magic wand that transforms the ordinary into the extraordinary. With each application, it's not just about coating the lashes; it's about creating a vision, a persona that's ready to take on Manhattan's streets. It's about finding the perfect wand that speaks to your style, be it volumizing, lengthening, or curling, each reflecting a different facet of the Manhattan dream.

➢ **The Art of Application**. Next, we delve into the nuances of mascara application, turning it into a ritualistic art. It's about the right strokes, the perfect angles, and the understanding that how you apply your mascara can change the entire narrative of your look. It's a ballet of brushes, where each movement is precise and intentional, designed to make the eyes not just seen, but felt.

➢ **The Color Palette of the City**. Consider the diverse range of mascara colors available, and how each shade can reflect a different aspect of Manhattan's multifaceted personality. From classic black to bold blues and mysterious greens, every color tells a story. It's about choosing a hue that not only complements your eyes but also echoes your mood and the city's ever-changing landscape.

➢ **The All-Weather Resilience**. In a city known for its unpredictability, from humid summers to windy autumns, your mascara should be as resilient as you are, a steadfast companion in

16

your Manhattan adventures. Consider choosing waterproof and smudge-proof options that ensure your lashes stay flawless, come rain or shine.

➤ **Layers of Drama**. We uncover the secrets of layering mascara to achieve the desired effect, from the understated elegance of a single coat to the bold drama of multiple layers—this is a balance between subtlety and boldness, understanding that in Manhattan, your lashes are a statement of your individuality and your mood.

➤ **The Finishing Touch**. The finishing touches make all the difference—the careful separation of lashes, the delicate touch-up that elevates the look from beautiful to breathtaking. It's about those final moments of refinement that mirror the city's own attention to detail and perfection.

➤ **The Manhattan Blink**. Finally, Unveiling the Mascara Craft ties it all back to the allure of the Manhattan Blink. It's about how, with the right mascara, every blink is a moment of communication, a silent language that speaks volumes. It's a reminder that in Manhattan, your lashes aren't just a part of your makeup; they're an essential component of your story, your personality, and your connection to the city.

In Unveiling the Mascara Craft, mascara isn't just makeup; it's a metaphor for the transformative power of beauty and the endless possibilities that Manhattan offers. It's about understanding that with the right touch, a simple blink can capture the essence of a city that's as vibrant and multifaceted as the people who walk its streets. This is where the craft of mascara becomes more than just a part of a beauty routine—it becomes a part of the Manhattan experience, a key to unlocking the city's heart and soul.

Your Triumphs: Mascara Craft Activities

Inspirational Quote

LET US MAKE OUR FUTURE NOW AND LET US MAKE OUR DREAMS TOMORROW'S REALITY. — Malala Yousafzai

Your Goals: Intentions and Thoughts

Beyond Beauty – Echoing Manhattan's Heartbeat

In Beyond Beauty—Echoing Manhattan's Heartbeat, we step beyond the superficial allure of aesthetics to discover how the true essence of beauty in Manhattan is intrinsically linked to the city's pulsating rhythm. This isn't merely about looking good; it's about embodying the spirit of the city through every sweep of mascara, every defined lash. It's where beauty transcends the mirror and becomes a reflection of the city's soul.

➤ **The Symphony of the Streets**. Here, we draw parallels between the rhythmic flutter of lashes and the vibrant beat of Manhattan's streets. Every blink resonates with the city's energy, from the hurried pace of Wall Street to the languid, dreamy afternoons in Central Park. It's about syncing your own rhythm with that of the city, letting your beauty echo the dynamic tempo of Manhattan life.

➤ **The Gaze of Aspiration**. In this part, we explore how the eyes can reflect the lofty aspirations and dreams that Manhattan is famous for. It's about capturing the glint of ambition, the sparkle of hope, and the depth of determination that characterizes the city's inhabitants. Your gaze becomes a window into your aspirations, mirroring the sky-reaching ambitions of the city's skyline.

➤ **The Reflection of Diversity**. Manhattan's beauty is in its diversity; here, we celebrate how each individual's unique beauty contributes to the city's mosaic. It's about embracing the myriad ways beauty is expressed and seen in the city, from the eclectic fashion of SoHo to the elegant charm of the Upper East Side. Every look, every set of lashes, tells a different story, adding to the city's rich tapestry of cultures and backgrounds.

➤ **The Whisper of Intimacy**. In a city that's always bustling, here we delve into the intimate moments that are shared through eye contact. It's about the soft, tender glances that cut through the city's noise, the shared looks that create private sanctuaries amid the chaos. These moments of intimacy are where the heart of Manhattan truly beats—in the quiet connections that happen in the midst of a crowd.

➤ **The Resilience in the Blink.** This part pays homage to the resilience that is mirrored in the eyes of those who call Manhattan home. It's about the strength and endurance reflected in a steady gaze, the undaunted spirit that's seen in the face of challenges. Your lashes aren't just framing your eyes; they're framing the resilience and unyielding spirit that the city instills in you.

➤ **The Dance of Light and Shadow.** Explore how the interplay of light and shadow in Manhattan is mirrored in the art of eye makeup. Just as the city basks in the brilliance of sunlight and the mystery of evening shadows, the way one highlights and contours their eyes can reflect these shifting moods. It's about using makeup to capture the ephemeral quality of light in Manhattan, from the golden hour glow to the neo-lit nights, and how these moments can be echoed in the depth and dimension of your gaze.

➤ **The Pulse of Seasonal Change.** In this point, we examine how the changing seasons in Manhattan influence the nuances of beauty routines. Just as the city transitions from the blossoming springs to the crisp autumns, the approach to beauty and especially eye makeup evolves. It's about embracing seasonal changes and allowing your makeup to reflect the city's transformation.

In Beyond Beauty—Echoing Manhattan's Heartbeat, beauty becomes more than skin deep. It transforms into a resonant echo of Manhattan itself, a mirror of the city's relentless energy, diverse cultures, shared intimacies, lofty dreams, and resilient spirit. It's an ode to how beauty, in all its forms, is interwoven with the very heartbeat of this iconic city, turning every glance, every blink, into a silent yet powerful testament to the essence of Manhattan.

Your Triumphs: Beyond Beauty Activities

_____

_____

_____

_____

_____

_____

_____

_____

_____

_____

_____

_____

_____

_____

_____

_____

_____

_____

_____

_____

_____

_____

_____

_____

Inspirational Quote

YOU DON'T ALWAYS NEED A PLAN. SOMETIMES YOU JUST NEED TO BREATHE, TRUST, LET GO, AND SEE WHAT HAPPENS. — Mandy Hale

Your Goals: Intentions and Thoughts

The Journey to Sky-High Lashes

In The Journey to Sky-High Lashes, we embark on an enchanting exploration through Manhattan's beauty scene, tracing the paths to achieving lashes that don't just flutter, but soar. This section isn't merely a guide; it's a narrative infused with the essence of Manhattan, capturing the allure, the mystique, and the vibrant spirit of the city, all through the lens of mastering the ultimate lash look.

> ➤ **The Quest Begins**. Our journey commences in the bustling streets of Manhattan, where the quest for the perfect lashes mirrors the city's relentless pursuit of dreams. Here, we navigate through the jungle of beauty salons and makeup counters, each offering their own version of the sky-high lash. It's a pilgrimage through the city's heart, a testament to the relentless search for beauty that defines Manhattan.

> ➤ **The Secret Salons**. We whisper about the clandestine salons tucked away in hidden corners of the city, where the art of lashes is elevated to a form of high art. These are the sanctuaries of beauty, where the city's elite come to transform their gaze. In these hallowed halls, the lash is more than just a feature; it's a statement, a declaration of one's presence in the city.

> ➤ **The Artisans of the Lash**. This section introduces the maestros of mascara, the architects of the arch, and the sculptors of the sweep. These are the artists who understand that every eye is a canvas, and every lash a stroke of genius. Their craftsmanship is a dance of precision and flair, reflecting the city's own blend of meticulous skill and bold creativity.

> ➤ **The Rituals and Potions**. We delve into the myriad of potions, serums, and techniques that promise to lift, curl, and lengthen. From the latest technological innovations to age-old natural remedies

passed down through generations, this is a treasure trove of secrets, each promising to elevate your lashes to new heights.

> **The Personal Touch of Customization**. Tailoring the lash experience to individual needs, preferences, and styles is not just a luxury in Manhattan, it's a necessity. This is where customization comes into play, from selecting the right type of mascara to choosing lash extensions or curling techniques. It's about creating a look that's not just on-trend but uniquely yours, reflecting your personality.

> **The Manhattan Blink Perfected**. The culmination of our journey is the perfect Manhattan Blink—a moment where style, sophistication, and seduction converge in a single flutter of the lashes. This blink is not just seen; it is felt. It carries the weight of the city's dreams, the depth of its stories, and the brightness of its lights.

> **The Reflection in the Mirror—and Beyond**. As we conclude our journey, it's about more than just the reflection in the mirror. It's about how those sky-high lashes are a reflection of the self, an embodiment of the city's limitless sky, its towering aspirations, and its boundless energy. In achieving these lashes, you become not just a part of Manhattan's landscape, but a defining feature of it.

In The Journey to Sky-High Lashes, we celebrate not just the beauty of the lashes themselves, but the journey to achieve them—a journey that is as much about self-discovery as it is about beauty. It's a narrative that intertwines the personal quest for the perfect lashes with the soul of Manhattan, a testament to the city's perpetual motion, its ever-evolving beauty scene, and its capacity to inspire and transform. This section is an ode to the magic that happens when the pursuit of beauty becomes an integral part of the Manhattan experience, where each bat of the lashes is a reminder of the city's grandeur and the dreams it holds.

BEHIND THE VELVET ROPE

Your Triumphs: Sky High Lashes Activities

Inspirational Quote

IF I CANNOT DO GREAT THINGS, I CAN DO SMALL THINGS IN A GREAT WAY.
— Martin Luther King Jr.

Your Goals: Intentions and Thoughts

Your Goals: Intentions and Thoughts

2

The Manhattan Mani-Pedi:
Nail the New York Chic, From Tips to Toes

Manhattan, a city where every corner pulses with an untamed beat, and even the smallest details matter, down to the polish on your nails. Here, it's not simply about embracing trends—it's about setting them. And in this land of ceaseless glamour, it's not just about having your nails done; it's about brandishing them as an extension of your very essence—with elegance, flair, and a flicker of the unexpected.

Now imagine: You're sauntering down Park Avenue, a latte in one hand, designer bag in the other. Every eye might be drawn to the sheen of your heels or the shimmer of your accessories, but it's the splash of color on your fingertips, and the impeccable finish on your toes, that truly spellbinds them. That, dear reader, is the Manhattan Manicure Majesty—a silent treatment to your impeccable taste, assertiveness, and the little quirks that make you, uniquely you.

In this tantalizing chapter of The Manhattan Diaries, we'll dive deep into the world of the city's manicure mystique. From the demure pastels that speak of Sunday brunches in Upper East Side to the audacious neon hues that scream downtown rooftop parties, you'll unravel how to wield your nails as the ultimate accessory.

But this isn't merely about color and gloss—no. It's about articulating the rhythm of a city that never sleeps, right from your fingertips to your toes. It's about capturing both the classic and the contemporary, tapping into the dual soul of Manhattan—one that's as timeless as Central Park in autumn, yet as edgy as a Brooklyn art show.

Join me, as we venture through clandestine nail bars and luxe salons, mastering the art of a mani-pedi that's not just a beauty ritual, but a statement. Because, darling, in Manhattan, every gesture, every subtle hand movement is an opportunity to dazzle. Ready your hands and feet, for the city beckons.

Welcome to The Manhattan Diaries—where your nails can echo the very spirit of this city, from its iconic skyscrapers to its hidden alleys.

The Manhattan Mani-Pedi

In The Manhattan Mani-Pedi, we delve into the art of manicures and pedicures that encapsulate the essence of Manhattan. This section explores how a simple mani-pedi transcends beauty, reflecting the city's vibrant energy through color choices and nail art. It's a journey through Manhattan's trend-setting nail bars, where each polish stroke and nail shape is a statement of personal style and an echo of the city's dynamic spirit. Here, every manicure and pedicure is not just grooming, but a wearable symbol of Manhattan's unique blend of timeless elegance and contemporary flair.

> **The Spellbinding Spectrum of Manhattan's Nail Palette.** This section captures the essence of Manhattan's dynamic and ever-evolving nail culture, blending the practical aspects of nail care with the poetic charm of the city, reminiscent of a leisurely Sunday brunch on the Upper East Side to the daring vibrancy of neon colors echoing the energy of downtown rooftop soirees, this point explores how nail colors are more than a choice; they're a statement of your persona and mood, reflecting the city's eclectic spirit.

> **Iconic Manhattan Manicure Moments.** This section delves into the history of nail trends set against the backdrop of Manhattan's fashion evolution. We'll recount iconic nail styles that have graced the avenues of this fashion capital, from classic reds to experimental art designs, and how these trends mirror the city's fashion milestones and cultural shifts.

> **Nail Bars and Luxe Salons: The Sanctuaries of Chic.** Journey through Manhattan's best-kept secrets—from hidden nail bars to opulent salons. Disco er where the city's style mavens go to get their

signature looks. This part of the chapter is not just about the places, but the experiences they offer, crafting a narrative about how these manicure havens are as much a part of the city's fabric as its iconic landmarks.

➤ **The Artistry of the Mani-Pedi Ritual**. Delve into the meticulous process of achieving the perfect Manhattan mani-pedi. From selecting the right shape to complement your hands, to the final glossy or matte finish, this point celebrates the ritualistic and artistic nature of nail care, showcasing it as an essential element of self-expression and style in the bustling city.

➤ **Manhattan at Your Fingertips: The Symbolism of Nails in the City Life**. Conclude by exploring how a well-done mani-pedi is more than just grooming; it's a form of communication, a way to articulate your identity and style. Discuss how every hand gesture, every step taken on the city's streets becomes an opportunity to showcase your unique flair, echoing the rhythm and heartbeat of Manhattan from your fingertips to your toes.

➤ **Seasonal Style Reflections**. Explore how Manhattan's mani-pedi trends shift with the seasons, from the pastel hues of spring to the rich, deep tones of winter, reflecting the city's trend-setting senses.

As we conclude our exploration of The Manhattan Mani-Pedi, it's clear that manicures and pedicures are more than just beauty treatments—they are vibrant expressions of Manhattan's spirit. Each color choice and nail design reflects the city's dynamic energy and diverse style. This section has shown us that in Manhattan, a manicure is not just grooming; it's a personal statement, a symbol of individuality, and an integral part of the city's fashion narrative. Whether making a gesture in a meeting or walking the city streets, your nails serve as a subtle yet powerful expression of New York's unique culture and rhythm.

Your Triumphs: Mani-Pedi Activities

Inspirational Quote

WE BECOME WHAT WE THINK ABOUT. — Earl Nightingale

THE MANHATTAN MANI-PEDI

Your Goals: Intentions and Thoughts

BEHIND THE VELVET ROPE

The Spellbinding Spectrum of Manhattan's Nail Palette

In The Spellbinding Spectrum of Manhattan's Nail Palette, we immerse ourselves in the vibrant and ever-changing world of nail color that epitomizes the essence of Manhattan. This is not just a chapter about choosing nail polish; it's a journey through the colors that paint the city's pulse, a spectrum that mirrors the diverse and dynamic spirit of New York.

> **The Whisper of Pastels**. Here, we explore the understated elegance of pastels, reminiscent of serene Sunday mornings in Central Park or leisurely brunches on the Upper East Side. These hues speak in soft tones, conveying a sophistication that's as subtle as it is powerful, mirroring the gentler side of the city's personality.

> **The Roar of Neons**. In stark contrast, we dive into the audacious world of neon polishes that scream with the energy of downtown Manhattan. These vibrant hues are a nod to the city's night owls, the trendsetters who turn the streets into their personal runways under the neon lights of rooftop bars and late-night diners.

> **The Classic Red**. This section pays homage to the timeless classic—the red nail. A color that's as iconic as the Empire State Building, red nails are a statement of confidence, a tribute to the city's enduring love affair with boldness and passion.

> **The Daring Dark Tones**. We then explore the deeper, more mysterious shades that resonate with the city's edgier side. These are the colors of Manhattan after dark, the hues that echo the mystery and allure of the city's hidden speakeasies and the secrets whispered in the shadows of its skyscrapers.

> **The Glitter and the Glam**. This section wouldn't be complete without a foray into the glittering world of metallics and shimmers. These polishes are the embodiment of Manhattan's dazzling skyline,

a reflection of the city's sparkle, from the glitzy theaters of Broadway to the twinkling lights of the Manhattan Bridge.

> **The Nudes and Neutrals**. Lastly, we touch upon the sophistication of nudes and neutrals. These shades are a nod to the city's professional heartbeat, the sleek, understated elegance that's as integral to Manhattan's identity as its more flamboyant colors.

> **The Whisper of Vintage Hues**. This segment delves into the nostalgic allure of vintage-inspired nail colors. From the muted tones of the 1920s to the vibrant hues of the 70s, these shades are more than just a nod to the past; they are a celebration of Manhattan's history, each color telling a story of a different era in the city's ever-evolving narrative.

> **The Boldness of Abstract Art**. Here, we explore the trend of nails as a canvas for abstract art. Inspired by the city's rich art scene, from the galleries of Chelsea to the street murals of Brooklyn, these designs go beyond conventional color choices.

> **The Elegance of Sheer and Translucent Tones**. This part highlights the allure of sheer and translucent polishes, a trend that mirrors the city's sophisticated side. These shades are like the sheer curtains of a penthouse overlooking Central Park—subtle, elegant, and with a hint of mystery, evoking a sense of understated luxury and refinement.

In The Spellbinding Spectrum of Manhattan's Nail Palette, we celebrate not just the hues themselves, but what they represent in the grand tapestry of New York life. Each color is a character, each shade a story, and together, they create a narrative as diverse and dynamic as Manhattan itself. This section is an ode to the power of color, and how, in the city that never sleeps, even the smallest details like the shade of your nail polish can speak volumes about who you are and the rhythm of the city you embody.

Your Triumphs: Nail Palette Activities

Inspirational Quote

BE YOURSELF, EVERYONE ELSE IS ALREADY TAKEN. — Oscar Wilde

THE MANHATTAN MANI-PEDI

Your Goals: Intentions and Thoughts

Iconic Manhattan Manicure Moments

In Iconic Manhattan Manicure Moments, we glide through the glamorous history of Manhattan's nail trends, each a glittering reflection of the city's ever-evolving fashion and cultural landscape. This chapter is not just a retrospective; it's a vivid tableau of the moments when manicures did more than just adorn fingertips—they made fashion statements, mirrored social shifts, and echoed the heartbeat of New York.

> ➤ **The Roaring Twenties Flapper Flair.** We begin our journey in the roaring twenties, where the flapper girls of Manhattan donned short, rounded nails painted in daring reds and deep plums. These bold colors were more than a fashion choice; they were a declaration of independence, a rebellion against the conventional, echoing the city's burgeoning spirit of freedom and flamboyance.

> ➤ **The Hollywood Glamour of the '50s and '60s.** As we twirl into the mid-century, we witness the rise of Hollywood's influence on Manhattan's manicure trends. The era of Marilyn Monroe and Audrey Hepburn brought with it a wave of chic, almond-shaped nails, often painted in classic reds or soft pinks. These manicures were a symbol of elegance and grace, mirroring the city's infatuation with the silver screen's glamour.

> ➤ **The Bold and Bright '80s.** Fast-forward to the 1980s, and we find ourselves amidst a burst of neon and glitter. In an era defined by bold fashion and louder music, Manhattan's nails were no less statement-making. Vibrant oranges, electric blues, and hot pinks adorned the hands of the city's trendsetters, a vibrant expression of the decade's go-big-or-go-home ethos.

> ➤ **The Minimalist '90s and the French Manicure Renaissance.** As the city sailed into the '90s, there was a shift to minimalism. The French manicure, with its clean lines and understated elegance,

became the embodiment of this era's chic simplicity. It was a manicure that whispered rather than shouted, yet still captured the essence of Manhattan's refined side.

➢ **The 2000s and the Rise of Nail Art**. With the turn of the millennium, Manhattan witnessed an explosion of creativity in nail art. Suddenly, nails became tiny canvases for intricate designs, from geometric patterns inspired by the city's architecture to sparkling embellishments that mirrored the city's night skyline. This era was about personalization and creativity, a reflection of Manhattan's endless capacity for innovation.

➢ **Today's Eco-Conscious and Health-Oriented Trends**. In today's Manhattan, the focus shifts towards eco-conscious and health-oriented manicures. This trend speaks to the city's growing awareness of sustainability and wellness, with a surge in organic polishes and treatments that promise beauty without compromise.

➢ **The DIY and Indie Movement of Recent Years**. Recently, there's been a surge in the DIY and indie nail movement, influenced by the city's burgeoning independent art and fashion scenes. This trend celebrates individuality and creativity, with more New Yorkers embracing at-home nail art, custom designs, and indie polish brands. It's a reflection of the city's entrepreneurial spirit and its celebration of personal style and innovation.

In Iconic Manhattan Manicure Moments, each chapter of the city's nail history is a snapshot of its broader story. It's a journey through time, where every manicure style reflects the shifting moods, trends, and spirits of Manhattan. From the flappers' rebellious reds to today's eco-friendly sheens, the evolution of the manicure is a vibrant narrative of the city itself, a city that continues to inspire and redefine the boundaries of beauty and style.

BEHIND THE VELVET ROPE

Your Triumphs: Manicure Moments Activities

_____

_____

_____

_____

_____

_____

_____

_____

_____

_____

_____

_____

_____

_____

_____

_____

_____

_____

_____

_____

_____

_____

_____

_____

Inspirational Quote

THE BAD NEWS IS TIME FLIES. THE GOOD NEWS IS YOU'RE THE PILOT. —
Michael Altshuler

THE MANHATTAN MANI-PEDI

Your Goals: Intentions and Thoughts

BEHIND THE VELVET ROPE

Nail Bars and Luxe Salons: The Sanctuaries of Chic

In Nail Bars and Luxe Salons: The Sanctuaries of Chic, we sweep into the exclusive and glamorous world of Manhattan's nail care havens, where the simple act of a manicure becomes an indulgent ritual of self-expression and style. This isn't just a section about where to get your nails done; it's a behind-the-scenes peek into the temples of beauty where Manhattan's chic elite go to be pampered, transformed, and to mingle with the city's trendsetters.

- ➤ **The High-Powered Nail Bars.** We start our tour in the bustling nail bars scattered across the city, each buzzing with the energy of Manhattan. These are not just salons; they're social hubs, places where deals are made, and gossip is traded as freely as stock tips on Wall Street. In these spaces, a manicure is an essential part of the power uniform, a subtle yet crucial element of the professional persona.

- ➤ **The Oases of Luxury.** Next, we glide into the opulent world of luxury salons. These are the sanctuaries where time seems to pause, a stark contrast to the city's relentless pace. Here, the manicure is elevated to an art form, with each treatment tailored to perfection, reflecting the salon's commitment to exclusivity and bespoke beauty.

- ➤ **The Trendsetting Boutique Salons.** In the heart of Manhattan's trendiest neighborhoods, we discover the boutique salons. These chic, intimate spaces are where the latest nail trends are born. Frequented by artists, fashionistas, and celebrities, these salons are incubators of creativity, blending traditional techniques with avant-garde styles, mirroring the city's ever-evolving fashion narrative.

- ➤ **The Secretive, Appointment-Only Spots.** We whisper about the almost mythical, appointment-only salons. Hidden away in unmarked spaces, these exclusive spots cater to a clientele for whom privacy is paramount. The experience here is about more than just luxury; it's about exclusivity and being part of an inner circle that's as elusive as the city's most hidden speakeasies.

➢ **The Holistic Wellness Retreats**. Venturing further, we encounter the holistic wellness retreats. In these serene spaces, a manicure is a part of a larger ritual of self-care and relaxation. Emphasizing organic treatments and eco-friendly practices, these salons cater to the New Yorker who seeks a sanctuary from the city's frenetic energy, a place where beauty aligns with wellness and sustainability.

➢ **The Vintage-Inspired Parlors**. Stepping into the world of vintage-inspired nail parlors, we find ourselves transported to a bygone era of elegance. These charming spots, with their retro décor and classic service, offer more than just a manicure; they provide a nostalgic escape, reminiscent of Old New York. Here, tradition meets style, as these salons revive time-honored nail care methods while infusing them with modern flair.

➢ **The Art Galleries of Nail Design**. Finally, we explore the salons that double as art galleries, where nail artists showcase their work like masterpieces. These spaces are a testament to the city's vibrant art scene, with walls adorned with innovative nail designs and color palettes. In these salons, clients don't just come for a manicure; they come for an artistic experience.

In Nail Bars and Luxe Salons: The Sanctuaries of Chic, each nail salon is a world unto itself, a reflection of the diverse facets of Manhattan's personality. From the high-energy nail bars to the tranquil retreats, these spaces are more than just places to get your nails done; they are the stages where Manhattan's beauty, power, creativity, and luxury play out, one polished fingertip at a time. This section is a tribute to the places that not only beautify but also capture the essence of the Manhattan lifestyle, where every manicure is a brushstroke in the grand painting of New York life.

BEHIND THE VELVET ROPE

Your Triumphs: Nail Bars and Salons Activities

Inspirational Quote

SPREAD LOVE EVERYWHERE YOU GO. — Mother Teresa

THE MANHATTAN MANI-PEDI

Your Goals: Intentions and Thoughts

The Artistry of the Mani-Pedi Ritual

In The Artistry of the Mani-Pedi Ritual, we step into the delicate and detailed world of nail care, a realm where each stroke of polish and snip of a nail is a testament to the meticulous craft that Manhattan has perfected. This section is not merely about painting nails; it's a deep dive into the ritualistic and almost ceremonial process that embodies the city's love affair with sophistication and style.

➢ **The Symphony of Preparation**. Our journey begins with the meticulous preparation, a symphony of steps to ensure the perfect canvas. Soaking, buffing, shaping—each action is deliberate, echoing the precision and attention to detail that Manhattan itself demands. This preparation is akin to the city's own rhythm, a careful setting of the stage before the main act.

➢ **The Palette of Possibilities**. We then waltz into the world of colors and textures. In Manhattan, a shade is never just a shade; it's a statement. The choice of polish—be it a classic red, a daring neon, or a subtle nude—is a reflection of mood, occasion, and personal style. It's about matching the pulse of your life to the color on your nails, a synchronization with the city's vibrant spectrum.

➢ **The Art of Precision**. Here, we delve into the artistry of application. The precision in painting each nail is akin to an artist delicately stroking paint onto a canvas. In Manhattan, where every detail is scrutinized, the way the polish is applied—smoothly, evenly, flawlessly—becomes a skill as revered as any artistic endeavor in the city's famed galleries.

➢ **The Mastery of Shape and Structure**. This section focuses on the critical aspect of shaping the nails, a skill where precision meets personal style. In Manhattan, the shape of your nails—be it the classic oval, the bold stiletto, or the trendy square—is as much a fashion statement as the shoes you choose. It's about finding the perfect contour that not only complements the hands but also aligns with one's lifestyle and fashion sensibilities, mirroring the city's architectural diversity.

> **The Innovation of Techniques and Tools**. Here, we explore the cutting-edge techniques and tools that keep Manhattan at the forefront of the mani-pedi artistry. From state-of-the-art UV lamps for flawless gel finishes to advanced nail strengthening treatments, this point highlights how innovation is continuously reshaping the mani-pedi experience, much like how technology continually transforms the cityscape.

> **The Personalization of the Experience**. Personalization can range from selecting a unique polish blend to bespoke nail art that reflects one's personality or even mood.

> **The Final Touches**. We then explore the final touches—the topcoats, the cuticle oils, the artful designs. These are the flourishes that elevate a simple manicure or pedicure to a fashion statement, a personal signature. It's the equivalent of the city's skyline lighting up at dusk, a transformation from the mundane to the magical.

> **The Ritual in the Routine**. Finally, we reflect on the ritualistic nature of the mani-pedi. In Manhattan, this routine is a cherished pause, a moment of luxury and self-care in the city's relentless pace. It's a personal ritual, a regular indulgence that, much like the city itself, is always evolving yet timeless in its appeal.

In The Artistry of the Mani-Pedi Ritual, we celebrate not just the aesthetic beauty of well-cared-for nails but the profound artistry and ritual embedded in their care. This chapter is a homage to the craft behind the gloss, the story behind each color, and the ritual in every routine—elements that encapsulate the elegance, precision, and flair of Manhattan itself.

BEHIND THE VELVET ROPE

Your Triumphs: Mani-Pedi Experience Activities

Inspirational Quote

DON'T WAIT. THE TIME WILL NEVER BE JUST RIGHT. — Napoleon Hill

THE MANHATTAN MANI-PEDI

Your Goals: Intentions and Thoughts

Your Goals: Intentions and Thoughts

Central Park Glow:
Natural Skin Care in the Urban Jungle

Manhattan, a city of soaring skyscrapers, shimmering lights, and unyielding determination. Here, it's easy to believe that the only way to thrive is with a cocktail of steel and stilettos. But beneath the bustling streets and beyond the dizzying heights, there lies a sanctuary—Central Park, an urban oasis where nature blooms amidst concrete. And it's in this juxtaposition that the true beauty of Manhattan emerges. It reminds us that amidst the urban, the natural can thrive—and so can our skin.

Now imagine: You're strolling down Madison Avenue, a gentle breeze rustling your hair. Eyes aren't just drawn to the chic silhouette of your ensemble or the glint of your jewelry, but the radiant glow of your skin—a complexion as fresh and vibrant as Central Park on a spring morning. That, my dear, is the Central Park Glow, a testament to the magic that occurs when the natural meets the urban, when organic skin care finds its rightful place in the heart of a bustling metropolis.

In this invigorating chapter of The Manhattan Diaries, we'll explore the hidden gems of holistic beauty nestled between New York's iconic landmarks. From the deep hydration of dew-kissed botanicals to the rejuvenating power of mineral-rich clays sourced from the city's very bedrock, you'll unearth the secrets to skin that not just survives, but thrives.

But this quest isn't only about serums and salves—oh no. It's about rediscovering a connection, a harmony with the city and its green heart. It's about realizing that the same park that offers respite to our souls can inspire solutions for our skin, harnessing the best of both worlds.

Join me, as we navigate this lush landscape, fusing the age-old wisdom of nature with the pulse of New York. And as we do, you'll learn that in Manhattan, every glance, every double-take is an affirmation of your natural beauty. So, darling, ready your skin, for the city—and its park—has tales to

51

tell and glow to bestow. Welcome to The Manhattan Diaries—where your natural radiance can shine as brightly as the city lights.

The Oasis of Central Park: Nature's Sanctuary in the Concrete Jungle

In the lush narrative of The Oasis of Central Park: Nature's Sanctuary in the Concrete Jungle, we delve into the art of harmonizing with nature's rhythms amidst Manhattan's urban beat, leaving a trail of mystique as enchanting as the park itself. It's about embodying the park's tranquil essence in a way that leaves an indelible imprint on the bustling cityscape.

➤ **The Whispering Leaves**. As you prepare to step out of Central Park's embrace, let the rustling leaves be your silent symphony. Their gentle whisper is a hint of untold secrets, a soft reminder of nature's enduring presence in the heart of the city, leaving others yearning to uncover the mysteries of this urban oasis.

➤ **The Half-Told Lore of the Park**. In your conversations, weave in tales of Central Park's hidden nooks and crannies, but leave them tantalizingly unfinished. Mention a secluded glade or a sun-dappled path, but don't divulge its location. Let these half-told stories of the park stir curiosity and imagination, inviting others to explore and discover its secrets for themselves.

➤ **The Glimpse of Natural Wonder**. Carry with you a small token from your park sojourn—a fallen leaf, a pebble, something that holds the essence of this natural retreat. This token is a subtle hint of your connection to the park, a small piece of its tranquility that you bring into the urban whirl, sparking intrigue about your bond with nature.

➤ **The Unanswered Question in Your Departure**. Leave your departure from the park shrouded in mystery. Making a passing comment about a serene moment or a chance encounter with wildlife, but let the details remain unsaid. This unanswered question about your experiences in the park will leave others intrigued, drawing them into the enigma of your connection with this natural haven.

➢ **The Hushed Goodbye to the Greens**. As you leave, let your farewell be a quiet, reflective moment, as if sharing a confidential goodbye with the park itself. This hushed farewell, laden with the serenity of nature, suggest a deeper, unspoken bond with the park, leaving those around you intrigued by the depth of your connection to this green sanctuary.

➢ **The Enigmatic Symbol of the Park**. Let a subtle, nature-inspired accessory be your silent statement—a leaf-shaped pendant, a floral scarf, an earth-toned piece that quietly speaks of your affinity for Central Park. This accessory invites curiosity and questions, a symbol of the park's mysterious allure that you carry with you.

➢ **The Unfinished Tale of Nature's Marvels**. Deliberately leave your anecdotes about the park's wonders incomplete. Start a story about a sunrise over the Bow Bridge or the autumn colors reflected in the Conservatory Water, but don't conclude it. This unfinished conversation invites others to ponder and wonder, drawing them into the allure of Central Park's natural beauty.

In The Oasis of Central Park: Nature's Sanctuary in the Concrete Jungle, it's not just about the journey through the park, but about the lasting impression it leaves. It's about ensuring that your connection with this natural haven isn't just a fleeting visit, but an ongoing narrative, a to-be-continued in the grand tale of your life in Manhattan. It's an art form, where each visit to the park is a carefully crafted scene, leaving a trail of mystique that weaves through your urban existence, long after you've left its green confines.

BEHIND THE VELVET ROPE

Your Triumphs: The Oasis of the Park Activities

Inspirational Quote

THE BEST AND MOST BEAUTIFUL THINGS IN THE WORLD CANNOT BE SEEN OR EVEN TOUCHED—THEY MUST BE FELT WITH THE HEART. — Helen Keller

Your Goals: Intentions and Thoughts

Unveiling the Natural Skincare Gems of Manhattan

In Unveiling the Natural Skincare Gems of Manhattan, we embark on a glamorous journey to discover the hidden treasures of Manhattan's natural skincare scene. Here's a glimpse into this world, where the essence of nature meets the allure of the city:

➤ **SoHo's Secrets Elixirs.** Venture into the heart of SoHo to uncover boutique stores brimming with natural skincare potions. Picture shelves lined with products whose ingredients have journeyed from exotic forests and distant mountains, each bottle a secret waiting to be whispered in the busy lanes of Manhattan.

➤ **Upper East Side's Luxurious Retreats.** Stroll along the pristine streets of the Upper East Side, where upscale spas offer indulgent treatments crafted from rare botanicals. These havens of tranquility promise rejuvenation, mirroring the serene pathways of Central Park, and are a favorite escape for those seeking a moment of peace in the city's fast-paced life.

➤ **The Chelsea Clean Beauty Revolution.** In the trendy neighborhood of Chelsea, discover minimalist stores that are at the forefront of the clean beauty movement. This is where eco-conscious Manhattanites gather, selecting products that not only nurture their skin but also care for the planet, reflecting the city's growing shift towards sustainability and wellness.

➤ **The Story Behind the Skincare.** Delve deeper into the tales woven into each natural skincare product. From rosehip oil supporting sustainable communities to clay masks born from a dermatologist's inspiration drawn from the city's green spaces, every item has a story as rich and diverse as Manhattan itself.

- ➢ **The Village's Vintage Apothecaries**. Wander into the quaint corners of Greenwich Village to discover vintage apothecaries, brimming with heritage beauty recipes that have been passed down through generations. These charming shops offer an enchanting blend of history and nature, where each jar and vial is filled with the wisdom of time-honored skincare traditions, reimagined for the modern Manhattanite.

- ➢ **Harlem's Organic Havens**. Journey uptown to Harlem where organic skincare shops celebrate the richness of natural ingredients favored in diverse cultures. Here, the community's vibrant spirit is captured in products that combine traditional herbal remedies with contemporary skincare needs, reflecting the neighborhood's rich cultural tapestry.

- ➢ **Brooklyn's Artisanal Beauty Bazaars**. Cross the bridge to Brooklyn, where artisanal markets and indie beauty workshops offer a treasure trove of handcrafted skincare delights. In these bustling bazaars, local artisans share their passion for organic beauty, offering bespoke products that capture the borough's eclectic energy.

- ➢ **Midtown's Luxury Green Beauty Boutiques**. In the heart of Midtown, uncover luxe boutiques that fuse opulence with eco-conscious beauty. These high-end stores offer a curated selection of natural skincare, where elegance meets ethical sourcing, catering to the discerning tastes of Manhattan's elite who seek luxury.

Unveiling the Natural Skincare Gems of Manhattan is not just about unearthing the city's natural beauty secrets; it's about exploring a world where the urban landscape and nature's gifts merge, creating a unique tapestry of skincare wonders. Each discovery is a nod to Manhattan's dynamic spirit, a celebration of the city where nature's touch adds to its undeniable charm and elegance.

BEHIND THE VELVET ROPE

Your Triumphs: Natural Skincare Gems Activities

_____
_____
_____
_____
_____
_____
_____
_____
_____
_____
_____
_____
_____
_____
_____
_____
_____
_____
_____
_____
_____
_____
_____
_____
_____
_____
_____
_____

Inspirational Quote

WHAT LIES BEHIND YOU AND WHAT LIES IN FRONT OF YOU, PALES IN
COMPARISON TO WHAT LIES INSIDE OF YOU. — Ralph Waldo Emerson

Your Goals: Intentions and Thoughts

The Science Meets Nature Approach

In The Science Meets Nature Approach, we embark on a thrilling journey where the brilliance of Manhattan's cutting-edge technology dances harmoniously with the timeless wisdom of natural skincare. Here's a glimpse of this captivating fusion, presented in a style that captures the essence of Manhattan's sophisticated allure.

> ➢ **Innovative Botanical Extractions**. Picture yourself in the laboratories where botanical treasures undergo a remarkable transformation. It's a delicate alchemy, a blend of the gardener's nurturing touch and the scientist's precision. Here, potent extracts are born, paving the way for serums and creams that are not only effective but also a beautiful metaphor for Manhattan's marriage of tradition and modernity.

> ➢ **High-Tech Hydration Techniques**. Dive into the world of cutting-edge hydration techniques. Manhattan's skincare experts harness the latest technology to lock in the precious moisture that nature provides. Imagine skincare products that borrow inspiration from cloud technology or employ micro-encapsulation to deliver hydration deep into your skin—much like the city itself, always finding innovative ways to thrive.

> ➢ **Customized Skincare Solutions**. Explore the realm of personalized skincare regimes, meticulously crafted through advanced diagnostics and algorithms. In a city that celebrates individuality, these bespoke solutions cater to your unique skin needs. They seamlessly blend natural ingredients with a scientific approach, creating a skincare cocktail as distinctive as you are.

> ➢ **Green Chemistry in Cosmetics**. Discover the pioneering work of green chemistry, where safer and sustainable methods reign supreme. Here, natural ingredients are extracted and preserved with

utmost care, mirroring Manhattan's commitment to innovation and sustainability. It's not just about enhancing your skin; it's also about safeguarding the environment.

> **Neuro-cosmetics and the Mind-Skin Connection**. Step into the fascinating realm of neuro-cosmetics, where skincare meets neuroscience. Products here aren't merely designed for physical benefits but also for their remarkable ability to elevate your mood and overall well-being. It reflects the city's holistic approach to beauty and health.

> **Age-Defying Biotechnology**. Explore the realm of age-defying biotechnology where cutting-edge research meets the wisdom of botanicals. Witness the creation of skincare products that harness the power of peptides, stem cells, and natural extracts to rejuvenate the skin, mirroring Manhattan's eternal quest for youth and vitality.

> **Nutricosmetics and Inner Radiance**. Uncover the concept of nutricosmetics, where beauty isn't just skin-deep. Manhattan's skincare enthusiasts embrace supplements and ingestible beauty products that enhance not only their outer appearance but also their inner radiance and well-being.

> **The Art of Natural Makeup**. Witness the rise of natural makeup that complements the glowing results of natural skincare. From clean cosmetics to makeup infused with botanical extracts, it's an artistic expression of Manhattan's desire for a flawless, yet au naturel, look.

In The Science Meets Nature Approach, we witness Manhattan's elegance and intelligence coming to life. It's a mesmerizing dance where groundbreaking scientific advancement elevate the pure essence of natural skincare. This captivating fusion echoes the city's unique flair for seamlessly melding the best of both worlds to create something truly extraordinary.

Your Triumphs: Science and Nature Activities

Inspirational Quote

WE KNOW WHAT WE ARE BUT KNOW NOT WHAT WE MAY BE. — William Shakespeare

CENTRAL PARK GLOW

Your Goals: Intentions and Thoughts

Lifestyle and Skincare Synergy

In the captivating world of Lifestyle and Skincare Synergy, where Manhattan's heartbeat orchestrates a mesmerizing blend of urban elegance and the art of caring for one's skin, we delve into the essence of this intriguing connection. Picture the city's elite, from the sleek streets to enchanting evenings, where each moment is an opportunity to showcase a radiant complexion. This is Manhattan's allure—a swift yet opulent dance between the rhythms of life and the pursuit of timeless beauty.

➢ **Urban Elegance**. Imagine the mornings of Manhattan's elite, a delicate ritual of skincare woven seamlessly into their fast-paced lives. It's a testament to the city's sophistication—a swift yet opulent moment of self-indulgence before plunging into the day's whirlwind.

➢ **From Day to Night**. Witness the transformation from the corporate boardrooms to the enchanting evenings, where the right skincare choice complements the transition from office chic to nightlife glamour. It's a skill every Manhattanite possesses, ensuring their skin radiates confidence in every setting.

➢ **Healthful Radiance**. Explore the connection between Manhattan's health-conscious lifestyle and its devotion to flawless skin. From yoga studios to green smoothie cafes, wellness is paramount, recognizing that inner vitality is the bedrock of external allure.

➢ **The Socialite's Secret**. Behold the allure of Manhattan's socialite, whose skincare regimen is as much a part of her social calendar as it is of her daily routine. From spa retreats to star-studded galas, she understands the transformative power of a luminous complexion.

➢ **A Global Melting Pot**. In a city that embraces diversity, skincare rituals from around the world converge. Manhattan's beauty landscape is a mosaic of cultural influences, where age-old remedies harmonize with modern innovations.

➤ **The Power of Rituals**. Dive into the private rituals of Manhattan's skincare enthusiasts, where applying lotions and serums is not just a task but a moment of self-connection. It's about savoring the act of self-care, an intimate gesture in the city that never stops.

➤ **Red Carpet Ready**. Discover the secrets behind the flawless complexions of Manhattan's celebrities and socialites. From pre-event facials to on-the-go touch-ups, it's a world where skincare professionals play a pivotal role in maintaining that coveted red-carpet radiance.

➤ **Beyond the Surface**. Explore the deeper connection between skincare and self-confidence. In Manhattan, skincare is not just about looking good; it's about feeling empowered. The city's residents understand that radiant skin is the canvas for their success stories, an embodiment of their inner strength.

➤ **The Night's Radiance**. Finally, bask in the glow that never dims— Manhattan's nocturnal charm. As the city comes alive at night, so does its skincare routine. Late-night serums and rejuvenating masks ensure that Manhattanites are always prepared for midnight adventures.

In the grand narrative of Manhattan's endless nights, Lifestyle and Skincare Synergy reveals the intimate synergy between the city's vibrant way of life and its timeless devotion to the art of skincare. It's a tale of choices, routines, and a city that inspires its residents to look and feel their best, no matter where the day—or night—may lead them. As you navigate this enchanting realm, remember that in Manhattan, beauty isn't just a reflection; it's an expression—a radiant ode to a life well-lived.

Your Triumphs: Lifestyle and Skincare Activities

_____
_____
_____
_____
_____
_____
_____
_____
_____
_____
_____
_____
_____
_____
_____
_____
_____
_____
_____
_____
_____
_____
_____
_____
_____
_____
_____
_____

Inspirational Quote

THINGS THAT WE LOVE TELL US WHAT WE ARE. — Thomas Aquinas

Your Goals: Intentions and Thoughts

Your Goals: Intentions and Thoughts

4

SoHo Salon Soirees:
Hair Dos and Don'ts with NYC's Top Stylists

Manhattan, a city where secrets aren't whispered, but rather styled into the tresses of its inhabitants. Here, every lock and curl narrates tales of late-night escapades, secret rendezvous, and dreams so vivid, they leave a trail of stardust on the avenues. This city doesn't merely see people—it feels their pulses, understands their desires, and gets intimate with their audacious aspirations.

Now picture this: There's a hint of dawn as you sashay down Spring Street. The world is drawn not to the brand of your heels or the sparkle of your earrings but by the sway of your freshly styled mane. That, my love, is the SoHo Salon signature—a style statement that mingles old-world glamour with downtown edge.

In this tantalizing chapter of The Manhattan Diaries, we venture into the dimly lit salons of SoHo, where magic happens at the hands of the city's most sought-after stylists. From the Bohemian waves that speak of a poet's soul to the sharp bob of a corporate queen. You'll learn the dos and the absolute don'ts of Manhattan hairstyling.

But its more than just hair—it's a manifesto. A SoHo Salon style is about embracing the city's contrasts, its grit, and its gleam. It's about wearing your stories, your victories, your heartbreaks, with pride and panache, letting each strand whisper tales of your adventures.

So, step into my world, where mirrors reflect more than just faces—they reveal destinies. Let's explore the salons that have seen countless transformations, from wide-eyed newcomers to seasoned city dwellers. Because, darling, in Manhattan, your hair isn't just an accessory—it's your anthology. Prepare to be transformed, for this city is ready to style not just your hair, but your soul. Welcome to The Manhattan Diaries—where your crown can shine as brilliantly as the city lights.

The Secret Life of SoHo Salons

In The Secret Life of SoHo Salons, the art of leaving a SoHo salon becomes a mesmerizing ballet of mystique, each exit as captivating and enigmatic as the streets of Manhattan itself.

➤ **The Enigmatic Smile**. As you step out of the salon, let your smile be a mysterious ode to the secrets shared and styles created within its walls. It's a smile that whispers of transformative conversations with your stylist, a silent narrative that leaves onlookers wondering about the tales woven into your hair.

➤ **The Half-Told Tale**. In your farewell, leave behind a half-told story of your salon experience. Hint at a whole new hair adventure or a stylist's secret tip, but let the details linger just out of reach, sparking curiosity and leaving a tantalizing air of mystery.

➤ **The Glimpse of a Secret**. As you gather your belongings, allow a hint of your new hairstyle to peek through—perhaps a uniquely placed hairpin or an unexpected streak of color. These subtle glimpses offer a teasing insight into your salon journey, compelling others to piece together the story of your latest look.

➤ **The Unanswered Question in Your Goodbye**. Depart with an open-ended remark about your next salon visit or a new style you're contemplating. Leave them pondering what's next in your hair saga, intrigued by the possibilities of your ever-evolving Manhattan style.

➤ **The Signature Scent**. Leave the salon with a signature scent that lingers in your hair, a mysterious and captivating aroma that becomes synonymous with your presence. This unique fragrance adds to the mystique of your persona, leaving a sensory impression that's as unforgettable as your style.

➢ **The Enigmatic Exit**. As you leave the salon, do so with an air of mystery, as if stepping into a new chapter. Your exit is not just the end of a salon visit but the beginning of a new narrative in the city's ever-unfolding story, leaving those around you intrigued about the next episode in your Manhattan saga.

➢ **The Unfinished Conversation**. Leave the salon with a conversation intriguingly open, an anecdote about your hair journey that you begin but don't conclude. This deliberate pause creates an allure, inviting others to wonder about the next chapter in your style story.

➢ **The Hidden Accessory**. Tuck a discreet, yet intriguing hair accessory into your style. It's a small piece, perhaps only partially visible, that hints at a story or a special significance, inviting curiosity and wonder about its origins and meaning.

➢ **The Style Evolution Tease**. Occasionally hint at your style's evolution, suggesting an upcoming change or a new direction in your look. This tease keeps your personal narrative dynamic and evolving, much like the city itself.

➢ **The Seductive Trail of Hair**. As you move through Manhattan, let your hair leave a seductive trail—a flow of locks that captures attention and stirs imagination. Your hair becomes a symbol of your journey through the city, a tangible reminder of your presence that lingers in the air.

In The Secret Life of SoHo Salons, every element of your salon experience—from the mysterious transformation to the elusive appointment—becomes a carefully crafted part of your enigmatic persona. It's an art form where your hair is not just styled but woven into the rich tapestry of Manhattan's mystique, leaving a trail of intrigue and allure that endures long after you've disappeared into the bustling streets.

BEHIND THE VELVET ROPE

Your Triumphs: Hair Salon Saga Activities

_____
_____
_____
_____
_____
_____
_____
_____
_____
_____
_____
_____
_____
_____
_____
_____
_____
_____
_____
_____
_____
_____
_____
_____

Inspirational Quote

THE MOST IMPORTANT THING IS TO ENJOY YOUR LIFE—TO BE HAPPY—
IT'S ALL THAT MATTERS. — Audrey Hepburn

Your Goals: Intentions and Thoughts

Stylist as Storyteller: Crafting Personal Narratives

In the heart of Manhattan, where the city's pulse beats strongest, lies the hidden world of SoHo's stylists—the unsung weavers of personal sagas in Stylist as Storyteller: Crafting Personal Narratives. Here, amidst the hum of dryers and the clink of scissors, these artisans don't just style hair; they craft stories, each strand a testament to the lives lived and dreams pursued in the city that never sleeps.

- ➤ **The Confessional Chair.** Step into the stylist's chair, a sacred space where whispered confessions and bold ambitions are woven into each cut. It's more than a seat; it's a haven where the secrets of the city are gently unraveled, and vulnerabilities are transformed into strength.

- ➤ **The Mirror as a Canvas.** In the reflection of the salon mirror, witness the transformation. Each snip, each color, is a stroke of genius, painting a portrait of the client's inner world. A new hairstyle here isn't just a change; it's an epiphany, a visual echo of personal growth and evolution.

- ➤ **The Intimate Bond.** Delve into the unique relationship between stylist and client, a bond forged over shared stories and mutual trust. This partnership is a dance of understanding and artistry, where the stylist interprets each client's narrative into a hairstyle that speaks louder than words.

- ➤ **The Transformation Tale.** Follow the journey of transformation that transcends the physical. From the shy first-timer seeking change to the regular seeking comfort in familiarity, each client leaves not just with a new look but with a renewed sense of self, their hair a bold declaration of who they are or aspire to be.

> ➤ **The Pulse of the City**. Discover how each hairstyle reflects the rhythm of Manhattan itself—the undying vibrancy, the eclectic mix of styles, and the ever-changing trends. In these salons, hair becomes a reflection of the city's soul, as diverse and dynamic as the streets themselves.

> ➤ **The Color of Emotion**. Explore how color becomes a language of its own in these salons. From the fiery reds echoing a bold new chapter to the soft pastels symbolizing a serene phase in life, stylists use color to narrate an emotional journey, painting feelings and experiences into every hue.

> ➤ **The Ritual of Renewal**. Delve into the salon visit as a ritual of renewal. It's not just about maintaining the hair; it's about rejuvenating the soul. Each appointment is a chance to shed the old and embrace the new, with stylists acting as guides in this transformative ritual.

> ➤ **The Legacy of Styles**. Discover the legacy of hairstyles that have passed through these salons. Each iconic cut or classic style carries a story from the past, a piece of Manhattan's history. Stylists here don't just create looks; they keep the city's rich legacy alive, one hairdo at a time.

In Stylist as Storyteller: Crafting Personal Narratives, we celebrate the stylists of SoHo, the silent narrators of New York's ever-evolving story. Each salon visit is more than a mere appointment; it's an entry into a world where hair is the medium, and life is the message. These stylists do more than change how we look; they transform how we see ourselves, weaving tales of resilience, beauty, and the unyielding spirit of Manhattan into every lock of hair. As you step back onto the bustling streets, your hair does more than catch the light—it tells your story, a story as captivating and unique as the city itself.

Your Triumphs: Hair Narrative Activities

_____

_____

_____

_____

_____

_____

_____

_____

_____

_____

_____

_____

_____

_____

_____

_____

_____

_____

_____

_____

_____

_____

_____

_____

_____

_____

_____

_____

_____

Inspirational Quote

IT IS DURING OUR DARKEST MOMENTS THAT WE MUST FOCUS TO SEE THE LIGHT. — Aristotle

Your Goals: Intentions and Thoughts

The Dos and Don'ts of Manhattan Hair

In the glittering cityscape of Manhattan, where style is a language unto itself, The Dos and Don'ts of Manhattan Hair serves as your essential guide to mastering the city's hair etiquette. This isn't just a chapter about hairstyles; it's a foray into the high-stakes world of New York fashion, where your tresses can speak louder than your Fifth Avenue ensemble.

- **The Art of Effortless Chic.** Embrace the dos of effortless elegance. Whether it's cascading waves that suggest a weekend escape to the Hamptons or a sleek chignon for a night at the Met, your hair should whisper tales of luxury and leisure, a perfect blend of carefree and carefully curated.

- **Precision Cuts for the City Life.** A sharp, precise cut is a definite do. It speaks of power lunches and high-stakes deals, a reflection of the city's skyline in its clean lines and angels. Think of the bob that's as sharp as your wit and as polished as your portfolio.

- **The Faux Pas of Overdoing.** Steer clear of the overdone. Over-teasing, over-styling, and over-accessorizing are the cardinal sins in Manhattan. Your hair should be a statement of sophistication, not a shout for attention.

- **The Signature Look.** Cultivate a signature style, a do that becomes synonymous with your persona. Whether it's an iconic curl or a bold color, let your hair be a hallmark of your unique identity, as recognizable as your signature on a cocktail napkin.

- **Adapting to Trends with Caution.** While keeping up with trends is a do, blindly following them without a nod to personal style is a definite don't. In Manhattan, the trendiest look is one that blends current fashions with your individual flair.

> **The Balance of Volume**. In Manhattan, the right amount of volume is a definite do. It's about achieving that perfect lift that speaks of brunches in chic cafes and rooftop cocktails—voluminous enough to make a statement, yet understated enough to maintain elegance. Over-the-top volume, however, can quickly venture into the territory of a don't, turning heads for all the wrong reasons.

> **The Subtlety of Highlights and Lowlights**. Subtle highlights and low lights are a do, offering a nod to the city's ever-changing light—from the golden hues of dawn over Central Park to the neon glows of Times Square at night. Overly dramatic streaks or unnatural colors, however, can clash with Manhattan's sophisticated palette, making them a fashion don't.

> **The Classic Look Revival**. Bringing back classic looks with a modern twist is a major do. Think Audrey Hepburn's timeless elegance reimagined for the 21st century—a style that says you respect the past but live fiercely in the present. However, clinging to outdated styles without a contemporary edge is a don't, as Manhattan is all about leading the trend, not living in the past.

> **Seasonal Hair Adjustments**. Adapting your hair to the seasons is a savvy do. Lighter tones and breezy styles for the summer, richer colors and fuller looks for winter—your hair should reflect the city's seasonal moods.

The Dos and Don'ts of Manhattan Hair is more than a mere guide to hair; it's a roadmap to thriving in the city's high-octane fashion scene. It's about understanding that in Manhattan, your hair is a symbol of your story, an accessory to your ambitions, and a testament to your place in the city's endless ballet of style and sophistication. As you navigate this world, remember that your hair is not just a part of you; in Manhattan, it can be your most powerful statement.

BEHIND THE VELVET ROPE

Your Triumphs: Hair Dos and Don'ts Activities

_____

_____

_____

_____

_____

_____

_____

_____

_____

_____

_____

_____

_____

_____

_____

_____

_____

_____

_____

_____

_____

_____

Inspirational Quote

REACH FOR IT. PUSH YOURSELF AS FAR AS YOU CAN. — Christa McAuliffe

Your Goals: Intentions and Thoughts

Hair as a Manifesto of Self-Expression

In Hair as a Manifesto of Self-Expression, we stride into the heart of Manhattan, a city where each hairstyle tells a story as compelling as the city's skyline. This section isn't merely about the latest trends in hair; it's an exploration into how every curl, cut, and color serves as a declaration of individuality, a narrative woven through the strands of one's hair, echoing the vibrant life of New York.

➤ **The Statement of Style.** Each hairstyle in Manhattan is a statement, a bold declaration of who you are. The tousled waves that speak of artistic flair, the sleek chignon that exudes sophistication, or the daring color that shouts your audacity—in Manhattan, your hair is your personal banner.

➤ **The Evolution of Self.** Hair in Manhattan reflects the evolution of self. It transforms with life's phases—the pie cut that marks a new beginning, the return to natural textures that signifies acceptance, or the adventurous colors that represent a journey into the unknown.

➤ **The Intimacy of the Salon Chair.** The salon chair in Manhattan is more than a seat; it's a confessional. Here, surrounded by the hum of dryers and the scent of shampoo, personal stories unfold, and transformations are not just of hair, but of souls.

➤ **The Trend-Setting Power.** Manhattanites don't just follow hair trends; they set them. From the runways to the streets, the styles born here resonate across the world, making each salon visit a potential genesis of the next big trend.

➤ **The Reflection of the City's Spirit.** Hair in Manhattan mirrors the city's spirit—diverse, dynamic, and ever-changing. It's as varied as the city itself, from the edgy cuts of Lower East Side to the polished styles of the Upper East Side.

➤ **The Symbolism of Length and Texture**. In Manhattan, the length and texture of your hair can symbolize a journey of self-discovery. Long, flowing locks might tell a story of romantic freedom, while a sharp, short cut could signify a bold new chapter in life. Embracing natural textures becomes a statement of authenticity, a nod to one's roots and heritage in the city that's a melting pot of cultures.

➤ **The Reinvention with Seasons**. Just as Manhattan shifts with the seasons, so does its hairstyles. The light, airy styles of summer, the rich tones of fall, the sleek looks of winter, and the fresh cuts of spring—each season brings a chance for reinvention, a rhythmic change that keeps pace with the city's heartbeat.

➤ **The Silent Conversation of Hair Accessories**. In Manhattan, hair accessories are not mere embellishments; they're part of the silent conversation about who you are. A vintage hairpin can whisper of nostalgia, while a futuristic hairpiece might shout about one's avant-garde tendencies, each accessory adding a layer to the story your hair tells.

➤ **The Unspoken Bond with Stylists**. The bond between Manhattanites and their stylists is profound, built on trust and understanding. A great stylist interprets your desires and fears, translating them into a style that's uniquely yours. This unspoken bond is a pivotal dance of creativity and understanding.

In Hair as a Manifesto of Self-Expression, hair transcends its traditional role, becoming a symbol of one's narrative in the ever-moving city of Manhattan. It's about embracing the transformative power of a haircut or color, about seeing your reflection in the mirror and knowing you're not just ready to take on the city but to tell your story, your way. In Manhattan, every strand, every curl, every hue is a chapter of your personal saga, a saga as captivating and unique as the city itself.

BEHIND THE VELVET ROPE

Your Triumphs: Hair Self-Expression Activities

_____

_____

_____

_____

_____

_____

_____

_____

_____

_____

_____

_____

_____

_____

_____

_____

_____

_____

_____

_____

_____

_____

_____

_____

Inspirational Quote

DON'T JUDGE EACH DAY BY THE HARVEST YOU REAP BUT BY THE SEEDS THAT YOU PLANT. — Robert Louis Stevenson

Your Goals: Intentions and Thoughts

Your Goals: Intentions and Thoughts

_____
_____
_____
_____
_____
_____
_____
_____
_____
_____
_____
_____
_____
_____
_____
_____
_____
_____
_____
_____
_____
_____
_____
_____
_____

Fifth Avenue Fragrances: Crafting Your Signature Scent Amidst City Scents

Manhattan, a city where the air is an intoxicating blend of dreams, desires, and dashes of daring. Every breath in this bustling metropolis tells tales of unbridled passion, hidden heartaches, and lingering love. And while navigating its streets, it isn't merely about reaching your destination; it's about leaving behind an essence that's uniquely you—with elegance, flair, and an air of mystique.

Imagine, as you swan down Fifth Avenue, a fragrant trail follows you, captivating and bewitching all in its wake. It's not the designer bag you clutch or the diamonds that drape you but the scent you wear. That, darling, is the true essence of the Manhattan Mystique, a sensory soiree that captures hearts and leaves an everlasting impression.

In this evocative chapter of The Manhattan Diaries, we dive nose-first into the world of Fifth Avenue Fragrances. From the intoxicating allure of vintage perfumeries to the avant-garde aroma labs crafting the future, you'll learn the art of concocting a scent that embodies your very soul.

But this journey isn't merely olfactory. It's about distilling the spirit of the city into a bottle, capturing its pulse, its rhythm, its fervor. It's about reflecting the dichotomy of Manhattan—a place where timeless elegance meets relentless ambition, where the nostalgic and the novel dance in harmony.

So come, let's waltz through the scented alleys of this city, discovering notes that resonate with our deepest desires and dreams. Because, sweetheart, in Manhattan, every spritz is a statement, a declaration of who you are and who you aspire to be. Prepare to leave a trail, for this city is ready to remember your essence. Welcome to The Manhattan Diaries—where your fragrance can be as enchanting as the city's aura.

BEHIND THE VELVET ROPE

The Allure of Vintage Perfumeries

In The Allure of Vintage Perfumeries, we delve into the enchanting corridors of Manhattan's past, tucked away in its vintage perfumeries. This section is a journey through time, where each scent is a story, and every bottle a relic of New York's glamorous history. Here, the aromas are not just fragrances; they are echoes of an era, a bridge to the city's bygone days of elegance and mystique.

- ➢ **Portals to the Past**. Step into these perfumeries, and you're stepping into history. The shelves are lined with bottles that are more than mere containers; they are portals, transporting you to the golden ages of Manhattan. Each scent is a tribute to a different era, from the bold and daring '20s to the refined and elegant '50s.

- ➢ **Scented Stories of Glamour**. These fragrances tell tales of old New York, a city of jazz, prohibition, and hidden speakeasies. They bring to life the stories of socialites and starlets, of grand balls and secret rendezvous, each aroma carrying whispers of the city's illustrious past.

- ➢ **The Art of Craftsmanship**. In these perfumeries, the art of fragrance is sacred. The craft is about precision and passion, blending notes to create scents that are timeless yet personal. It's a meticulous process, preserving the legacy of fragrance-making that has been passed down through generations.

- ➢ **A Personal Journey through Scents**. Finding your fragrance in these vintage stores is a personal odyssey. It's about connecting with a scent that speaks to you, that resonates with your story, and becomes a part of your own legacy in the tapestry of Manhattan.

- ➢ **Echoes of Iconic New Yorkers**. Each scent in these perfumeries carries echoes of iconic New Yorkers—from artists and writers to socialites and stars. Discover fragrances that might have graced the likes of Audrey Hepburn or Truman Capote, lending an air of classic sophistication and timeless charm to your own persona.

➢ **The Romance of Rare Ingredients**. Unearth the allure of rare, almost forgotten ingredients—a whiff of orris root or a hint of Mysore sandalwood. These perfumeries are treasure troves of exotic and scarce components, each adding a layer of depth and uniqueness to your signature scent.

➢ **The Legacy of Perfume Bottles**. Admire the artistry of the perfume bottles themselves, each a piece of history. From intricately designed flacons to simple, elegant, vials, these bottles are as much a testament to the era's craftsmanship as the fragrances they hold.

➢ **The Ritual of Fragrance Discovery**. Experience the ritual of discovering your fragrance—a personal journey that involves more than just the sense of smell. It's about the feel of the bottle, the story behind the scent, and how it aligns with your essence and the city's spirit.

➢ **Scent as a Time Capsule**. Each visit to a vintage perfumery is like opening a time capsule. Whether it's a scent that recalls the roaring '20s or the swinging '60s, you're not just choosing a perfume; you're choosing a piece of time, a fragment of history that resonates with your soul.

The Allure of Vintage Perfumeries is more than just a chapter about fragrances; it's an homage to the timeless elegance of Manhattan, captured in the essence of perfumes. These stores are not merely shops; they are sanctuaries of history, where the city's heart beats in every bottle. As you emerge back onto the bustling streets, the fragrance you carry is not just a scent; it's a piece of New York's soul, a personal emblem of the city's enduring allure and your place within its never-ending story.

BEHIND THE VELVET ROPE

Your Triumphs: Signature Scent Activities

Inspirational Quote

PERFECTION IS NOT ATTAINABLE, BUT IF WE CHASE PERFECTION, WE CAN CATCH EXCELLENCE. — Vince Lombardi

FIFTH AVENUE FRAGRANCES

Your Goals: Intentions and Thoughts

Avant-Garde Aroma Labs

Avant-Garde Aroma Labs whisks us away into the heart of Manhattan's innovative scent scene, where the essence of the city's relentless innovation is captured in the art of modern perfumery. This chapter isn't merely about discovering new fragrances; it's an odyssey into the spaces where the boundaries of traditional scent-making are pushed, creating a world where each aroma is a bold statement of New York's ever-evolving character.

➢ **The Alchemists of Aroma.** Enter the world of the avant-garde perfumers, modern-day alchemists who blend unconventional ingredients with a touch of Manhattan's flair. In these labs, traditional floral notes are infused with urban edge—think concrete accords, metallic hints, and rain on the city streets, crafting scents that defy expectations.

➢ **The City as Inspiration.** Witness how the city itself becomes a muse in these aroma labs. Every scent is a homage to New York— from the leafy tranquility of Central Park to the electric buzz of Times Square, the perfumers distill the essence of these experiences into innovative and expressive fragrances.

➢ **Sensory Experimentation.** Step into a realm of sensory experimentation, where visitors are encouraged to explore and interact with fragrances in ways that transcend the traditional. It's a space where scent is not just smelled but felt and experienced, mirroring the city's dynamic and immersive spirit.

➢ **The Birthplace of Trends.** Discover how these aroma labs are the birthplaces of the next big trends in perfumery. Here, what starts as a daring experiment in a SoHo loft can become the next global fragrance phenomenon, setting the tone for what the world wears.

➢ **Personalized Scent Journeys**. Delve into the personalized scent journeys offered by these labs. Beyond off-the-shelf perfumes, these labs provide bespoke fragrance experiences, tailoring scents to individual stories and personalities, much like the city tailors dreams to those who dare to chase them.

➢ **Fusion of Technology and Scent**. Discover the cutting-edge technology that's reshaping the world of fragrance in these labs. From scent capsules that change with your mood to perfumes that are personalized based on genetic makeup, these innovations are blurring the lines between science and scent, much like Manhattan blends the lines between dream and reality.

➢ **Sustainability in Scent Creation**. Learn about the emphasis on sustainability in these labs. Conscious and ethical sourcing of ingredients, eco-friendly packaging, and green chemistry methods are as integral to these perfumes as their enchanting aromas, mirroring Manhattan's growing commitment to environmental responsibility.

➢ **The Cultural Melting Pot in a Bottle**. Explore how these avant-garde perfumeries capture the essence of Manhattan's diverse cultural tapestry. Scents are infused with notes from around the world, paying homage to the city's rich multicultural heritage and the myriad of stories and traditions that converge in its bustling streets.

In Avant Garde Aroma Labs, we explore the frontiers of fragrance, where each scent is a bold declaration of the city's innovative spirit. This section is a celebration of the new and the unexpected, an ode to the city that constantly reinvents itself and inspires those within it to do the same. In these labs, perfume is not just a fragrance; it's an expression of the city's soul—as daring, diverse, and vibrant as Manhattan itself.

Completed Tasks: Aroma Lab Activities

Inspirational Quote

THE BEST PREPARATION FOR TOMORROW IS DOING YOUR BEST TODAY. —
H. Jackson Brown Jr.

FIFTH AVENUE FRAGRANCES

Action Items: Intentions and Thoughts

The Essence of Manhattan in a Bottle

In The Essence of Manhattan in a Bottle, we embark on a fragrant odyssey to encapsulate the very soul of New York City within the confines of a perfume bottle. This section is not merely about concocting a scent; it's a narrative woven with the essence of Manhattan's streets, parks, rivers, and the indefinable energy that pulses through them. It's a quest to distill the city's aura into an olfactory masterpiece.

- ➤ **Capturing the City's Rhythms**. The essence of Manhattan is its rhythm—the bustling streets, the quiet mornings in Central Park, the energetic nights. Perfumers seek to capture these rhythms, blending notes of urban vigor with whispers of natural tranquility, creating a fragrance that dances to the beat of the city.

- ➤ **The Diversity of Aromas**. From the aromatic complexity of a street market in Chinatown to the crisp ocean breeze of the Hudson, the city's diverse aromas are its signature. Each scent is a thread in the city's rich tapestry, contributing to a fragrance that is as multifaceted as Manhattan's own cultural mosaic.

- ➤ **The Challenge of Balance**. Just as Manhattan balances its skyscrapers with its green spaces, perfumers balance a myriad of scents to create a harmonious fragrance. It's about finding equilibrium—a scent that can embody the city's chaos and serenity in equal measures.

- ➤ **A Scent of Aspiration and Memory**. The final fragrance is one that evokes not just the present city but its past and future. It holds the aspirations of those who come to Manhattan seeking dreams and the memories of those who have walked its streets, a scent that tells a story of ambition, nostalgia, and unending possibility.

➢ **The Scent of Architectural Majesty**. Incorporate the scents inspired by Manhattan's architectural wonders—the stony grandeur of the Empire State Building, the sleekness of modern skyscrapers, and the historical richness of the Art Deco district. These notes add a structural and majestic quality to the fragrance, mirroring the city's skyline.

➢ **Seasonal Whispers of the City**. Capture the changing seasons of Manhattan in the scent. The fresh blossoms of spring in the Botanical Gardens, the warm summer air wafting from Central Park, the crispness of fall leaves in Riverside Park, and the cold, invigorating whiff of winter snow—each season brings its unique aroma to the blend.

➢ **Nocturnal Notes of New York**. Channel the city's vibrant nightlife into the fragrance. Notes that evoke dimly lit jazz clubs, the buzz of neon lights in Times Square at midnight, and the sultry allure of a Manhattan night add a mysterious and enigmatic layer to the perfume.

➢ **Olfactory Ode to Manhattan's Culinary Scene**. Infuse hints of the city's diverse culinary scene—a dash of spices from a curry in Little India, the sweetness of a cannoli in Little Italy, or the smokiness of street food vendors. These scents pay homage to the city's rich and diverse gastronomic landscape.

The Essence of Manhattan in a Bottle is a journey through the sensory landscape of one of the world's most iconic cities. In trying to capture its essence, perfumers engage in a romance with the city, interpreting and reinterpreting its scents until they have a fragrance that doesn't just mimic Manhattan but embodies it. Wearing this perfume is like carrying a piece of the city's soul with you, a constant reminder of the endless stories and dreams woven into the fabric of Manhattan.

Your Triumphs: Soul in a Bottle Activities

_____

_____

_____

_____

_____

_____

_____

_____

_____

_____

_____

_____

_____

_____

_____

_____

_____

_____

_____

_____

_____

_____

_____

_____

_____

_____

Inspirational Quote

ABSORB WHAT IS USEFUL, REJECT WHAT IS USELESS, ADD WHAT IS SPECIFICALLY YOUR OWN. — Bruce Lee

Your Goals: Intentions and Thoughts

BEHIND THE VELVET ROPE

Fragrance as a Personal Statement

In Fragrance as a Personal Statement, we delve into the intimate and evocative world of scent within the bustling streets of Manhattan. Here, each fragrance is more than just a blend of notes; it's a reflection of one's innermost self, a scented signature that tells a story more compelling than any outfit or accessory. This section is a journey into the heart of personal expression, where the choice of perfume becomes a profound declaration of individuality and style in the city that never sleeps.

> ➤ **The Essence of Identity**. In Manhattan, your fragrance is an extension of your identity. It's the spicy note that speaks to your daring side, the subtle floral hint that whispers of your elegance, or the fresh, clean scent that tells of your love for simplicity. Each choice is a piece of the puzzle that is you.

> ➤ **The Ritual of Selection**. Choosing a fragrance in New York is a sacred ritual, a moment of introspection and discovery. It's about navigating through the myriad scents until you find the one that resonates with your soul—the scent that feels like coming home.

> ➤ **A Symphony of Moods**. Just as Manhattan is a city of diverse moods and moments, your fragrance wardrobe is a symphony of expressions. It changes with your emotions, your goals, and the rhythms of your life—a dynamic and ever-evolving olfactory diary.

> ➤ **The Power of Memory**. Fragrance has the power to evoke memories and create new ones. In a city brimming with stories, the scent you wear can transport you back to precious moments or accompany you as you make new memories, each spritz a chapter in your personal narrative.

> ➤ **The Statement of Independence**. In a city where independence is celebrated, wearing a unique fragrance is a statement of self-reliance

and confidence. It's about breaking free from the trends, finding your scent, and owning it—much like carving your own path in the city.

➢ **The Signature of Seasons**. In the ever-changing landscape of Manhattan, your fragrance adapts to the seasons. The light, floral scents of spring, the bold and bright tones of summer, the rich, earthy notes of fall, and the crisp, clean aromas of winter—each season brings its own scented statement, reflecting the city's transformation throughout the year.

➢ **The Whisper of Evening Wear**. The choice of fragrance for the night is a whispered secret of seduction and sophistication. The evening scents are more daring, more provocative—a reflection of Manhattan's glittering nightlife, where every outing is an opportunity to be someone a little more mysterious, a little more enchanting.

➢ **The Comfort of Familiarity**. Amidst the chaos of city life, a familiar fragrance can be a comforting anchor. It's the scent you return to time and time again, the one that feels like an old friend—reassuring, constant, and unmistakably yours.

➢ **The Scent as a Social Statement**. In the social tapestry of New York, your fragrance can be a statement of your beliefs and values. For example, the scent you wear can speak volumes about what you stand for—cruelty-free brands, supporting local perfumers, etc.

Fragrance as a Personal Statement is more than just a guide to choosing a perfume; it's an exploration of how scent can be a powerful tool of expression in the dynamic landscape of Manhattan. It's about the confidence that comes from wearing a fragrance that perfectly captures your essence, and the allure of leaving a trace of yourself in the air as you navigate the city. In Manhattan, a fragrance is not just what you wear; it's who you are, as integral to your persona as your words, your actions, and your dreams.

Your Triumphs: Choosing a Perfume Activities

Inspirational Quote

LIFE HAS GOT ALL THOSE TWISTS AND TURNS. YOU'VE GOT TO HOLD ON TIGHT AND OFF YOU GO. — Nicole Kidman

Your Goals: Intentions and Thoughts

Your Goals: Intentions and Thoughts

6

Red Lips and Broadway Hips:
Finding the Perfect Shade for Every City Occasion

Manhattan, the city where every blink is a flirtation and every smile is a story. Here, one's stride down its avenues isn't just movement—it's a statement. And while the buildings rise to kiss the skies, it's the lips of its inhabitants that truly tell tales of desires, dreams, and dalliances. And what, might you ask, is the weapon of choice for these tales? A shade of red, powerful enough to stop traffic and bold enough to define destinies.

Imagine, your steps synchronized with the city's heartbeat, as you sashay down Fifth Avenue. Eyes aren't just tracing the hem of your ensemble but are entranced by the fiery hue gracing your lips. That, my dear, is the true power of the Manhattan Kiss—a statement, an attitude, a proclamation of self.

In this tantalizing chapter of The Manhattan Diaries, we dive into the realm of reds. From the audacious crimson of a Broadway diva to the soft blush of a Central Park sunset, you'll unveil the art of selecting the shade that not just suits, but defines you.

Yet, this is not merely about cosmetics. It's about capturing the essence of every corner, cafe, and cabaret in the city. It's about wearing the very pulse, drama, and allure of Manhattan on one's lips. A dance between vulnerability and vigor, coyness and courage.

So, accompany me as we trace the contours and curves of the city, learning to reflect its shades on our lips. Because, darling, in Manhattan, a pout isn't just pretty—it's potent. Gear up to set the stage on fire, for the city is ready to be seduced by your story. Welcome to The Manhattan Diaries—where your lip shade is as legendary as the city's legacy.

The Power of the Manhattan Kiss

In the city that never sleeps, The Power of the Manhattan Kiss reigns supreme. It's about capturing the essence of every corner, cafe, and cabaret, where every pout is potent. From the audacious crimson of a Broadway diva to the soft blush of a Central Park sunset, it's the art of selecting the defining shade. Embrace The Manhattan Kiss, where every kiss tells a legendary story, setting the stage on fire and leaving an indelible mark on Manhattan's legacy.

➤ **The Iconic Red**. In the heart of Manhattan, the iconic red lip reigns supreme. It's the classic crimson that echoes the sophistication of the Upper East Side, capturing the essence of timeless beauty that transcends trends and time itself.

➤ **Selecting Your Signature**. Unveil the art of selecting the shade that not just suits, but defines you. Your lip shade is your signature in a city where every detail matters.

➤ **Broadway Drama**. Venture into the realm of Broadway with deep, sultry reds that embody the passion and drama of the city's iconic theater district. Your lips become the leading role, commanding attention and applause wherever you go.

➤ **Rooftop Romance**. Feel the romance of a Manhattan rooftop soiree as you embrace shades that mirror the mesmerizing sunset over the city skyline. These hues whisper of whispered promises and stolen moments.

➤ **Jazz-Inspired Tones**. Immerse yourself in the sultry melodies of Harlem's jazz clubs with lip shades that capture the rhythm and soul of the city's vibrant music scene. Your lips become a symphony of style and sophistication.

➤ **Central Park Serenity**. Find tranquility in soft, muted reds that reflect the serene beauty of Central Park in the early morning. Like a leisurely stroll through the park, these shades exude calmness and natural elegance.

➢ **Downtown Edge**. Embrace the downtown vibes with edgy, unconventional red shades that reflect the artistic and avant-garde spirit of neighborhoods like SoHo and Greenwich Village. Your lips become a canvas for self-expression and rebellion.

➢ **Corporate Chic**. Explore sophisticated red hues that align with the polished, corporate world of Wall Street. These shades convey authority, ambition, and a touch of sensuality, making them perfect for business meetings and power lunches.

➢ **Fashion Week Reds**. Channel the glamour of New York Fashion Week with bold and daring reds that push the boundaries of style. These statement shades demand attention and turn heads wherever you go, just like the fashionistas on the runway.

➢ **Cocktail Hour Elegance**. Transition seamlessly from the office to cocktail hour with versatile red lip colors that exude elegance and charm. These shades are perfect for after-work soirees, adding a touch of allure to your evening.

➢ **The Pulse of Manhattan**. Understand that it's not simply about cosmetics; it's about wearing the pulse, drama, and allure of the city on your lips. Your pout becomes a potent weapon, captivating and alluring.

In the world of Manhattan, your lips hold the power to enchant, captivate, and leave a lasting impression. They become a canvas for your unique story, an expression of your confidence and charisma. So, embrace the Power of the Manhattan Kiss and let your lips become a part of the city's rich tapestry, where every kiss is an unforgettable tale of allure and passion.

Your Triumphs: The Manhattan Kiss Activities

_____

_____

_____

_____

_____

_____

_____

_____

_____

_____

_____

_____

_____

_____

_____

_____

_____

_____

_____

_____

_____

_____

_____

_____

_____

_____

Inspirational Quote

OUT OF DIFFICULTIES GROW MIRACLES. — Jean de la Bruyere

Your Goals: Intentions and Thoughts

BEHIND THE VELVET ROPE

Shades that Define Manhattan Moments

In the heartbeat of Manhattan, where every moment is a scene waiting to unfold, the right shades on your lips can be your script. Each shade paints a different story, defines a unique Manhattan moment, and captures the essence of this dazzling city. Join me as we explore the art of choosing lip shades that do more than enhance your beauty—they define your Manhattan moments.

➢ **Classic Red Elegance**. Start your Manhattan journey with the timeless allure of classic red lip shades. Channel the sophistication of a night at the opera or a romantic dinner at a candlelit bistro. These shades exude confidence and poise, making them perfect for those quintessential New York moments.

➢ **Rooftop Romance Pinks**. As the sun sets over the city skyline, embrace the romance of rooftop soirees with soft, dreamy pink lips shades. These hues capture the magic of Manhattan evenings, where love and laughter fill the air. Your lips become a canvas of affection, painting moments to remember.

➢ **Bold Broadway Berries**. Venture into the vibrant world of Broadway with bold berry lip shades that demand the spotlight. Whether you're attending a dazzling musical or exploring the city's theater district, these shades command attention and mirror the city's electric energy.

➢ **Uptown Chic Nudes**. Discover the understated elegance of uptown chic with nude lip shades that evoke the sophistication of Upper East Side galleries and upscale brunches. These shades are the epitome of understated glamour, allowing your natural beauty to shine through.

➢ **Sultry Sunset Corals**. Capture the essence of Manhattan's breathtaking sunsets with sultry coral lip shades. These colors embody the warmth of a city that never sleeps, perfect for rooftop cocktails and waterfront strolls along the Hudson River.

➢ **Chinatown Spice Vibes**. Immerse yourself in the vibrant energy of Manhattan's Chinatown with spicy lip shades that reflect the flavors and aromas of this bustling neighborhood. These shades add a touch of excitement to your look, ideal for exploring cultural festivals and street markets.

➢ **Central Park Serenity**. Experience the tranquility of Central Park with serene mauve lip shades that echo the park's lush greenery and serene lakes. These colors bring a sense of calm to your style, perfect for picnics and leisurely walks in the heart of the city.

➢ **Financial District Power**. Embrace the power and ambition of Manhattan's Financial District with bold and authoritative lip shades. These hues exude confidence and determination, suitable for important business meetings and career-defining moments.

➢ **East Village Bohemian**. Dive into the artistic spirit of the East Village with bohemian lip shades that reflect the neighborhood's creative vibes. These colors are a nod to the avant-garde and eclectic, perfect for exploring art galleries and live music venues.

In this journey through Shades that Define Manhattan Moments, remember that your choice of lip color is more than a cosmetic decision—it's a statement, a mood, and a reflection of the moment you want to create. Your lips become a brush, painting your Manhattan moments with the most vibrant and evocative colors. So, embrace the power of shades and let your lips narrate the stories of your unforgettable Manhattan adventures.

Your Triumphs: City Moment Shades Activities

_____
_____
_____
_____
_____
_____
_____
_____
_____
_____
_____
_____
_____
_____
_____
_____
_____
_____
_____
_____
_____
_____
_____
_____
_____
_____
_____
_____
_____

Inspirational Quote

NO ACT OF KINDNESS, NO MATTER HOW SMALL, IS EVER WASTED. — Aesop

Your Goals: Intentions and Thoughts

The Art of Selecting the Perfect Red

In the heart of Manhattan, where every glance carries a story, choosing the ideal red lipstick isn't just about makeup—it's a statement of self. As you navigate the city's pulse, your lips, painted in the perfect shade of red, become a captivating narrative without words. This is The Art of Selecting the Perfect Red—a journey through Manhattan's allure, where every hue is a brushstroke on your life's canvas.

- ➤ **Sultry Scarlet Seduction**. Delve into the world of sultry scarlet shades, a passionate and bold choice that mirrors Manhattan's fiery spirit. These reds are for nights at rooftop bars overlooking the city's skyline, where sparks fly as you sip cocktails and exchange glances with intriguing strangers.

- ➤ **Classic Manhattan Crimson**. Embrace the timeless elegance of classic Manhattan crimson, reminiscent of the city's iconic red doors. This shade is your go-to for sophisticated evenings at Broadway shows or upscale restaurants, where you make a statement without uttering a word.

- ➤ **Brick Red Bohemian Vibes**. Explore the bohemian side of Manhattan with brick red hues that capture the artistic soul of the city. These shades are your companions for gallery openings in Chelsea and poetry readings in the West village, where creativity knows no bounds.

- ➤ **Downtown Burgundy Edge**. Dive into the downtown burgundy edge, reflecting the edginess of neighborhoods like SoHo and the Lower East Side. These daring reds are your choice for underground concerts and warehouse parties, where you're the embodiment of avant-garde allure.

- ➤ **Uptown Ruby Refinement**. Bask in the uptown ruby refinement, inspired by the opulence of the Upper East Side. These shades adorn your lips for charity galas and museum galas, where you grace the city's elite gatherings with your presence.

- ➤ **Whispering Rose Twilight**. Step into the subtle elegance of whispering rose twilight, a soft, muted red that speaks to serene early evenings in Central Park. This shade is perfect for those reflective strolls by Bethesda Terrace or romantic boat rides on the lake, where the city's hustle fades into gentle whispers.

- ➤ **Fiery Soiree Fuchsia**. Ignite your nightlife with fiery soiree fuchsia, a vibrant and playful red with a pink undertone that captures the exhilarating beat of Manhattan's club scene. Wear it to dance the night away in trendy nightclubs or to lively, impromptu street festivals in the East Village.

- ➤ **Metropolitan Merlot Mystery**. Embrace the sophisticated and mysterious allure of metropolitan merlot mystery, a deep, rich burgundy that pairs well with the enigmatic ambiance of Manhattan's exclusive wine bars and speakeasies. This color is a nod to the hidden gems and secretive locales that only the true city dwellers know.

- ➤ **Highline Cherry Charm**. Celebrate the vibrant life and restoration of the High Line with highline cherry charm, a bright and cheerful cherry red. This shade is ideal for daytime adventures along the elevated park, complementing the panoramic views of the Hudson.

In the art of selecting the perfect red, Manhattan's vibrant pulse finds its echo. Each shade is a stroke of creativity, a testament to the myriad facets of your persona, and a reflection of the city's multifaceted charm. As you choose your red, remember that it's not just a color—it's an ode to the city that never sleeps, an affirmation of your unique story, and a brush with destiny.

Your Triumphs: Shades of Red Activities

_____

_____

_____

_____

_____

_____

_____

_____

_____

_____

_____

_____

_____

_____

_____

_____

_____

_____

_____

_____

_____

_____

Inspirational Quote

A PLACE FOR EVERYTHING, EVERYTHING IN ITS PLACE. — Benjamin Franklin

Your Goals: Intentions and Thoughts

Lips that Speak Manhattan

In the heart of Manhattan, where every glance carries a story, choosing the ideal lip shade isn't just about makeup—it's a statement of self. As you navigate the city's pulse, your lips, painted in the perfect shade, become a captivating narrative without words. This is the art of Lips that Speak Manhattan—a journey through the city's allure, where every hue is a brushstroke on your life's canvas.

- ➤ **The Bold Red**. Like the flashing marquees of Broadway, a bold red lip commands attention and exudes confidence. It's the shade for conquering the city, leaving a mark wherever you go.

- ➤ **The Soft Blush**. Reflecting the gentle hues of a Central Park sunset, a soft blush lip whispers of romance and tranquility. It's perfect for those intimate moments in the city's quieter corners.

- ➤ **The Vibrant Coral**. Vibrant and full of life, a coral lip mirrors the energy of Manhattan's bustling streets. It's the go-to shade for daytime adventures and rooftop soirees.

- ➤ **The Mysterious Berry**. As enigmatic as a hidden speakeasy, a deep berry lip hints at secrets and intrigues. It's the choice for those who embrace the city's hidden alleys and clandestine affairs.

- ➤ **The Elegant Nude**. Like the classic lines of Manhattan's skyscrapers, an elegant nude lip exudes sophistication. It's ideal for business meetings and high-society soirees.

- ➤ **The Daring Plum**. Channel the mysterious and bold energy of Manhattan's avant-garde theater scene with daring plum. This deep, provocative shade is perfect for evening performances or an artistic gathering in the eclectic neighborhoods of the Lower East Side.

- ➤ **The Classic Taupe**. Reflecting the sleek, urban aesthetics of Wall Street's polished stone and steel, classic taupe is a subtle yet powerful choice. Ideal for navigating the professional mazes of the financial district with a touch of class.

➢ **The Bright Pink Pop**. Embrace the spirited vibe of Times Square with bright pink pop, a shade as lively and dynamic as the area's flashing neon lights and bustling crowds. It's the perfect companion for standing out in the city that demands to be noticed.

➢ **The Rich Expresso**. Inspired by the aromatic coffee culture of Greenwich Village, rich espresso offers a deep, comforting brown town that speaks to leisurely mornings in quaint cafes and spirited discussions in local bookstores. It's a shade for the intellectual and chic urbanite.

➢ **The Gleaming Gold**. Capture the luxurious essence of Fifth Avenue shopping with gleaming gold. This opulent shade is perfect for browsing high-end boutiques or attending a glamorous gallery opening, adding a touch of undeniable luxury and prestige.

➢ **The Sassy Magenta**. Reflecting the vibrant spirit of Chelsea's art scene, sassy magenta is a bold and expressive choice that matches the creative pulse of the neighborhood's famed art galleries and lively nightlife.

➢ **The Smoky Quartz**. Drawing from the mysterious allure of Manhattan by moonlight, smoky quartz is a sultry, deep gray with a hint of shimmer. It's the ideal choice for late-night jazz clubs in Harlem or a sophisticated evening stroll along the Hudson River.

In a city that never sleeps, your lips can narrate the chapters of your life. Each shade is a page-turner, each moment a plot twist, and together, they compose the epic tale of your Manhattan journey. Let your lips speak the language of the city, for they are the storytellers of your adventures, desires, and dreams.

Your Triumphs: Lip Shade Chapters Activities

Inspirational Quote

I HATED EVERY MINUTE OF TRAINING, BUT I SAID, "DON'T QUIT. SUFFER NOW AND LIVE THE REST OF YOUR LIFE AS A CHAMPION." — Muhammad Ali

Your Goals: Intentions and Thoughts

Your Goals: Intentions and Thoughts

7

Bronzed in Brooklyn: Tanning Secrets for that Year-Round City Sunshine

Brooklyn, a borough not just sketched with the dreams of those who traverse its streets, but painted with the deep hues of their passions, intrigues, and raw New York spirit. Across the East River, as Manhattan's sister and rival, it holds its ground with the edgy elegance. And amidst its historic brownstones and eclectic boutiques, the truest accessory is not your chic handbag, but the radiant glow that exudes from your sun-kissed skin.

Imagine: The sun over the Brooklyn Bridge, casting the city in a golden hue, and there you are, strolling through DUMBO, your bronzed skin capturing the last rays of light, making you the talk of the waterfront. Sweetheart, that's the Brooklyn Bronze—a sunlit aura so captivating it might as well have been kissed by Brooklyn's own sun.

In this tantalizing chapter of The Manhattan Diaries, we delve deep into the art of achieving that ethereal glow. Whether you're gracing the hipster cafes of Williamsburg or the vintage stores of Bushwick, these secrets ensure you're not just seen, you're remembered.

But this bronzed beauty isn't merely skin deep. It's the manifestation of the soul of Brooklyn—a blend of its historic charm and modern vibrancy. It's about basking in the glory of both its past and present, shining brighter with every bridge you cross.

Join me, as we journey from the sun-soaked beaches of Coney Island to the bustling avenues of Flatbush, seeking the secrets to that perfect Brooklyn Bronze. After all, in this borough, every ray of sunshine is an invitation to dazzle. Strap on those sandals, darling, and let's chase that Brooklyn sun together. Welcome to The Manhattan Diaries—where your glow rivals the city lights.

The Brooklyn Glow: Radiate with Sun-Kissed Brilliance

In the heart of Brooklyn, where each street tells a story, achieving the perfect year-round tan isn't just a beauty routine—it's an art form. As you wander through the borough's diverse neighborhoods, your bronze skin becomes a canvas, showcasing your sunlit radiance amidst the backdrop of brownstones and boutiques.

- ➤ **The Brooklyn Glow**. Explore the techniques to attain that quintessential Brooklyn glow, a sun-kissed aura that captures the essence of the borough's vibrant energy. It's not just about tanning; it's about embracing the spirit of Brooklyn and wearing it with pride.

- ➤ **The Secrets of Sunscreen**. Discover the importance of sun protection in maintaining a healthy and long-lasting tan. From choosing the right SPF to understanding the nuances of sunscreen application, these secrets ensure that your bronzed beauty remains flawless and radiant.

- ➤ **The Art of Self-Tanning**. Dive into the world of self-tanning and learn the tips and tricks to achieve a perfect tan at any time of the year. Whether it's for a special occasion or to keep that Brooklyn bronze in the winter months, self-tanning is your go-to technique.

- ➤ **Brooklyn's Beauty Spots**. Uncover the hidden gems of Brooklyn, from the scenic waterfronts to the cozy parks, where you can soak up the sun and enhance your bronzed allure. These beauty spots not only offer the perfect tanning backdrop but also a slice of Brooklyn's unique charm.

- ➤ **The Confidence of a Brooklyn Bronze**. Embrace the confidence that comes with a radiant tan. Your tan isn't just about aesthetics; it's about feeling empowered and ready to conquer the world. Let your glow be a reflection of your inner strength and vitality.

➢ **Golden Hour Secrets**. Uncover the magic of the golden hour, when the Brooklyn sun bathes everything in a warm, ethereal glow. Learn how to capture the perfect bronzed look during this enchanting time of day.

➢ **Local Eateries and Tanning Spots**. Explore the charming cafes and hidden tanning spots in Brooklyn where you can savor delectable treats while working on your tan. It's a delightful fusion of gastronomy and bronzing.

➢ **Bronzed and Bohemian**. Dive into the world of Brooklyn's bohemian culture and discover how your bronzed glow perfectly complements the artistic and free-spirited atmosphere of this borough.

➢ **Brooklyn Nights and Your Radiance**. Explore the nightlife of Brooklyn and experience how your bronzed skin becomes a stunning accessory under the neon lights and starry skies of this vibrant city.

➢ **Seasonal Tan Trends**. Stay ahead of the curve by mastering the seasonal tan trends that sweep through Brooklyn. From the deep, rich tones favored in autumn to the light, golden hues that sparkle in summer; understanding these trends will ensure your tan is always in style and reflects the seasonal vibes of the borough.

In a borough as diverse as Brooklyn, your tan becomes a testament to your adventurous spirit and your ability to shine amidst the urban landscape. It's not just about bronzing your skin; it's about bronzing your soul with the vibrant essence of Brooklyn. Let the sun be your guide as we explore the secrets of that perfect Brooklyn bronze, because in this borough, every ray of sunshine is an opportunity to shine.

Your Triumphs: Bronze Glow Activities

_____

_____

_____

_____

_____

_____

_____

_____

_____

_____

_____

_____

_____

_____

_____

_____

_____

_____

_____

_____

_____

_____

_____

_____

Inspirational Quote

EVEN IF I KNEW THAT TOMORROW THE WORLD WOULD GO TO PIECES, I WOULD STILL PLANT MY APPLE TREE. — Martin Luther

Your Goals: Intentions and Thoughts

The Secrets of Sunscreen

In the dazzling world of beauty, where every glow tells a tale and every complexion whispers secrets, there's one unsung hero that reigns supreme: sunscreen. The magic of a radiant visage often begins with the diligent application of this elixir of youth. But it's not just about protection; it's about indulgence, about the daily ritual of self-love that leaves you not just guarded but also luminous. So, join me on this sun-kissed journey through the Secrets of Sunscreen, where we'll uncover the mysteries of maintaining your glow while basking in the city's endless sunshine.

➢ **The Sun-Kissed Canvas**. Sunscreen isn't just a shield; it's the canvas upon which your radiant beauty is painted. It's the foundation of your daily ritual, the first step to a day filled with allure and magnetism. Embrace this canvas, for it's where your journey to luminosity truly begins.

➢ **Guardian of Youth**. Beyond its immediate protection, sunscreen is the guardian of your youthful allure. It shields you from the relentless march of time, ensuring that your skin remains a testament to the city's vibrant energy. Think of it as a sentinel, standing guard over your beauty through the years.

➢ **A Ritual of Self-Love**. Applying sunscreen is not just a practicality; it's a daily ritual of self-love. It's a moment of indulgence, a whisper of care that leaves you feeling cherished, and it's a declaration that your allure is worth preserving. Let each application be a love letter to yourself.

➢ **The Luminous Shield**. Think of sunscreen as your luminous shield against the city's brilliant rays. It's your secret weapon, allowing you to bask in the brilliance of the city while ensuring your skin remains forever kissed by the sun. Embrace this shield, for it's your path to eternal radiance.

➢ **A Fountain of Confidence**. Sunscreen isn't just about protecting your skin; it's about boosting your confidence. Knowing that you're shielded from the sun's harmful effects allows you to step out into the world with a radiant glow and the assurance that your allure remains intact.

➢ **City-Proof Beauty**. In the bustling city, where every day is an adventure, sunscreen is your secret weapon to maintain city-proof beauty. It shields your skin from the urban elements, ensuring that pollution and environmental stressors don't dull your luminosity.

➢ **The Ageless Elixir**. Sunscreen is the ageless elixir that defies time. It's a timeless investment in your beauty, allowing you to look back at the years and see not just the memories you've made but also the ageless allure that has remained constant.

➢ **An Everyday Luxury**. Consider sunscreen an everyday luxury, a moment of pampering in the midst of your busy city life. It's a touch of opulence that elevates your daily routine and reminds you that self-care is the ultimate indulgence in the world of beauty.

➢ **Harmony with Hydration**. Elevate your sunscreen ritual by pairing it with hydrating serums and moisturizers that boost its efficacy. This synergy not only enhances sun protection but also ensures your skin remains plump and dewy throughout the day. It's a dual action that fortifies your skin's barrier and amplifies its glow, making your sunscreen routine a cornerstone of holistic skin health.

In the world of skincare, sunscreen isn't just a shield; it's the key to maintaining your luminous allure. Let these Secrets of Sunscreen be your guide, allowing you to bask in the city's brilliance while keeping your skin forever kissed by the sun. Embrace the ritual, for in each drop of sunscreen, you'll find the essence of beauty, allure, and self-love.

Your Triumphs: Daily Sunscreen Ritual Activities

Inspirational Quote

BRAND YOURSELF FOR THE CAREER YOU WANT, NOT THE JOB YOU HAVE.
— Dan Schawbel

Your Goals: Intentions and Thoughts

The Art of Self-Tanning

In the heart of the city that never sleeps, where glamour and sophistication meet at every street corner, there's an art form that every Manhattanite swears by—The Art of Self-Tanning. In a place where first impressions matter and where confidence is the ultimate accessory, achieving the perfect tan isn't just a beauty ritual; it's a statement. Imagine stepping out of your Upper East Side apartment, your skin kissed by the golden glow of a Manhattan sunset. Heads turn, and you exude the kind of radiance that leaves a lasting imprint on the city's memory. That, darling, is the Manhattan Tan—a sunlit embrace of your inner allure, a testament to your cosmopolitan charm.

➢ **The Golden Elixir.** Discover the finest self-tanning products that promise a flawless, streak-free tan. It's like bottling the essence of a Manhattan summer and applying it to your skin, ensuring you radiate warmth and confidence year-round.

➢ **The Art of Application.** Learn the precise techniques that turn self-tanning into a work of art. From the gentle sweep of the tanning mitt to the meticulous blending around the elbows and knees, it's a ritual that rivals the city's most exquisite performances.

➢ **Choosing Your Shade.** Just as you select the perfect dress for a night out in Manhattan, choosing the right tan shade is an art. Whether it's a sun-kissed bronze or a deep, sultry glow, your tan should be an expression of your personal style.

➢ **Maintaining the Glow.** The Manhattan Tan doesn't fade; it evolves. Explore the maintenance rituals that keep your tan looking as fresh as the city's energy. From hydrating lotions to extending mists, it's all about preserving the allure.

➢ **The Tan-Worthy Events.** Explore the occasions and events in Manhattan where showcasing your radiant tan is an absolute must.

From rooftop soirees to Broadway premiers, discover where your Manhattan Tan can steal the spotlight.

➢ **The Celebrity Tanning Tips**. Learn from the best in the business as we uncover the self-tanning secrets of Manhattan's celebrities and influencers. What do they swear by to achieve that coveted Manhattan glow?

➢ **Tanning Dos and Don'ts**. Navigate the nuances of self-tanning etiquette in the city. Discover the common mistakes to avoid and the must-follow rules to ensure your tan always looks impeccable.

➢ **The Empowerment of Tan**. Beyond the aesthetics, understand the empowering feeling that comes with a flawless tan. How does the Manhattan Tan boost your confidence and make you feel ready to conquer the city's challenges?

➢ **Seasonal Tan Adjustments**. Master the art of seasonal tan adjustments to perfectly sync with Manhattan's changing climates and fashion trends. Learn how to lighten your tan for the sparkling snowfalls of winter or enrich it for the lush greenery of summer, ensuring your skin's glow is always in harmony with the season.

➢ **Eco-Conscious Tanning Choices**. Discover the latest advancements in organic and vegan self-tanners.

But this isn't just about achieving a flawless tan; it's about embodying the spirit of the city itself—an intoxicating blend of elegance, confidence, and allure. Join me as we continue to unveil the secrets of self-tanning that have graced the skin of Manhattan's elite. After all, in this city, every day is an opportunity to shine, and your tan should be nothing less than iconic. Get ready to embrace the warmth of the Manhattan Tan, for it's more than a shade; it's a lifestyle. Welcome to The Manhattan Diaries—where your radiant tan is as unforgettable as the city's skyline.

Your Triumphs: Self-Tanning Activities

_____

_____

_____

_____

_____

_____

_____

_____

_____

_____

_____

_____

_____

_____

_____

_____

_____

_____

_____

_____

_____

_____

_____

_____

_____

_____

Inspirational Quote

GIVE LIGHT AND PEOPLE WILL FIND THE WAY. — Ella Baker

Your Goals: Intentions and Thoughts

Brooklyn's Beauty Spots

Brooklyn, the borough that serves as a canvas for dreams and an incubator for artistic souls. Amidst its diverse neighborhoods and eclectic streets, you'll find an array of hidden gems and beauty spots waiting to be discovered. This is Brooklyn's Beauty Spots, where creativity meets charisma, and authenticity is the ultimate adornment.

- ➤ **The Neighborhood Nooks**. Uncover the charming beauty salons and spas nestled within Brooklyn's neighborhoods. From the vintage-inspired parlors in Williamsburg to the serene retreats in Park Slope, each enclave offers a unique beauty experience that mirrors the spirit of its locale.

- ➤ **Artistry in Brooklyn's Boutiques**. Step into the world of boutique skincare and makeup shops that line the streets of DUMBO and Cobble Hill. These carefully curated spaces showcase independent beauty brands and artisans who add their touch of Brooklyn magic to every product.

- ➤ **Nature's Beauty Haven**. Explore the lush green spaces and parks where you can embrace the beauty of nature in the heart of the city. From the Brooklyn Botanic Garden to Prospect Park, these natural sanctuaries provide a serene backdrop for self-care and relaxation.

- ➤ **Brooklyn's Beauty Icons**. Meet the local beauty entrepreneurs and influencers who have made their mark in the industry. Discover their inspiring stories and learn how they've harnessed the borough's creative energy to redefine beauty standards.

- ➤ **The Artisan Perfumeries**. Venture into the charming world of artisanal perfumeries that call Brooklyn home. These fragrance ateliers craft unique scents inspired by the borough's diverse neighborhoods. From the spicy notes of Bed-Stuy to the fresh sea breeze of Sheepshead Bay, each fragrance captures the essence of Brooklyn's dynamic personality.

➢ **Graffiti Glamour**. Brooklyn's street art scene isn't just confined to walls—it's become a part of the beauty culture. Discover the innovative makeup artists who draw inspiration from graffiti and street murals. They incorporate bold colors and artistic designs into their makeup looks, blurring the lines between makeup and art.

➢ **Brooklyn's Wellness Retreats**. Indulge in wellness retreats that offer holistic beauty treatments and relaxation experiences. These havens in Gowanus and Red Hook combine ancient healing practices with modern skincare to rejuvenate your body and soul. Unwind with yoga sessions, organic facials, and massages that leave you refreshed and revitalized.

➢ **The Fashion Forward**. Brooklyn has its own unique fashion sense, and it's reflected in the beauty choices of its residents. Explore the boutiques and salons where you can get the latest Brooklyn-inspired hairstyles and nail art. From trendy barbershops in Bushwick to avant-garde nail studios in Greenpoint, you'll find beauty services that keep you in vogue.

In the heart of Brooklyn's Beauty Spots, you'll encounter a world where creativity knows no bounds. Whether it's the scents that transport you to different neighborhoods, the makeup that becomes a form of expression, the wellness retreats that nurture your inner glow, or the fashion-forward trends that redefine beauty, Brooklyn has it all. Embrace the diversity, vibrancy, and individuality that make Brooklyn's beauty truly exceptional. It's an ode to self-expression and the pursuit of beauty that knows no limits.

BEHIND THE VELVET ROPE

Your Triumphs: Tanning Salon and Spa Activities

Inspirational Quote

IF I HAVE SEEN FURTHER THAN OTHERS, IT IS BY STANDING UPON THE SHOULDERS OF GIANTS. — Isaac Newton

Your Goals: Intentions and Thoughts

The Confidence of a Brooklyn Bronze

Brooklyn, a borough as diverse as its inhabitants, is a place where self-expression reigns supreme. In the midst of its bustling streets and artistic enclaves, there's a common thread that weaves through the lives of its residents—the confidence that comes from sporting a radiant Brooklyn bronze. This isn't just a tan; it's a statement, a badge of honor that signifies a life well-lived in this vibrant city. Join me as we delve into the allure of the Brooklyn bronze, exploring the secrets behind the confidence it bestows.

> ➤ **The Brooklyn Bronze Ritual.** In Brooklyn, achieving the perfect bronze isn't just about vanity; it's a ritual. Residents take pride in maintaining their sun-kissed glow year-round. From carefully selecting the right self-tanner to the precise application techniques, it's a process that's both meticulous and meditative. The act of self-tanning becomes a cherished routine, a moment of self-care that sets the tone for the day.

> ➤ **The Radiance of Self-Assuredness.** Sporting a Brooklyn bronze isn't just about aesthetics; it's about embodying self-assuredness. The confidence that comes from knowing your skin looks and feels its best is a powerful asset in a city known for its fast pace and high expectations. Whether you're navigating the entrepreneurial scene of DUMBO or mingling in the art galleries of Bushwick, that radiant bronze serves as a silent reminder of your inner strength and resilience.

> ➤ **The Social Signature.** In Brooklyn, your tan isn't just a personal choice; it's a social signature. It's a conversation starter, an invitation to connect with fellow bronzed enthusiasts. Whether you're bonding over brunch in Williamsburg or sharing stories at a rooftop gathering in Gowanus, your Brooklyn bronze becomes a shared experience, creating connections that go beyond skin-deep.

- ➢ **The Brooklyn Confidence Effect**. The Brooklyn bronze isn't just skin-deep; it's a mindset. It's the assurance that you can conquer the challenges of city life with grace and poise. It's the knowledge that you belong in a place where individuality is celebrated, and self-expression is an art form. The confidence it instills isn't just about appearance; it's about embracing life with an open heart and an unwavering spirit.

- ➢ **The Wellness Connection**. Embrace the wellness aspect of achieving a Brooklyn bronze. This radiant glow is not just about beauty; it's also about health and well-being. Engage in activities like yoga in the park or jogging along the Brooklyn Bridge, where the natural sunlight enhances your tan and boosts your vitamin D levels, contributing to a holistic sense of health and vitality.

- ➢ **Fashion and Flair**. Discover how the Brooklyn bronze complements the borough's eclectic fashion scene. Learn how a sun-kissed glow can accentuate your style choices, from bohemian dresses to sharp, tailored suits. Your tan can be the perfect accessory to highlight bold patterns and colors, making every outfit pop with more vibrance and confidence.

- ➢ **Seasonal Celebrations**. Tailor your Brooklyn bronze for seasonal festivities and celebrations. From summer barbecues in Prospect Park to winter holiday parties in trendy loft spaces, adjust your tan's intensity to suit the occasion, no matter the season.

In the heart of Brooklyn, amidst its diverse neighborhoods and artistic enclaves, the confidence of a Brooklyn bronze thrives. It's more than a tan; it's a symbol of resilience, self-expression, and the unwavering belief that you can shine brightly in this vibrant borough. So, embrace the Brooklyn bronze, not just as a beauty choice, but as a lifestyle—a reflection of the unwavering confidence that defines the spirit of Brooklyn.

BEHIND THE VELVET ROPE

Your Triumphs: Bronze Social Signature Activities

_____

_____

_____

_____

_____

_____

_____

_____

_____

_____

_____

_____

_____

_____

_____

_____

_____

_____

_____

_____

_____

_____

_____

Inspirational Quote

CLOUDS COME FLOATING INTO MY LIFE, NO LONGER TO CARRY RAIN OR USHER STORM, BUT TO ADD COLOR TO MY SUNSET SKY. — Rabindranath Tagore

Your Goals: Intentions and Thoughts

Your Goals: Intentions and Thoughts

8

Midnight Facials and East Side Tales: Nighttime Rituals of the City's Elites

Manhattan, a city that doesn't merely embrace the night—it becomes one with it, revealing in the moonlight the whispered secrets, forbidden rendezvous, and ageless beauty rituals of its dazzling denizens. Amidst its luminescent skyline, it's not just about ending one day and starting another; it's about the magic that unfolds when the city sleeps and the elite play.

Now imagine: You're emerging from one of the Upper East Side's exclusive spas, a midnight moon casting a glow on your rejuvenated skin, turning heads not due to the brand of your heels, but the allure of your refreshed countenance. Darling, that's the Manhattan Midnight Magic—a beauty regime so transformative, it could be mistaken for moonlit alchemy.

In this alluring chapter of The Manhattan Diaries, we venture behind the golden doors of the city's most secretive beauty havens. From rejuvenating jade rollers and glistening gold masks to serums made of dreams and whispers, you'll unearth the rituals that keep the city's elites glowing from dusk till dawn.

But this isn't just about skin-deep splendor. It's about aligning with the city's pulsating energy, about refreshing not just the face, but the soul. It's about tapping into Manhattan's ageless spirit, allowing both the glamour and the mystery to seep into your very pores.

Join me, as we navigate the starlit streets and clandestine corners, immersing ourselves in the beauty rites that aren't just transformative, but utterly enchanting. Because, in this city, every evening offers a canvas for rejuvenation and every dawn a revelation of its mastery. Slip into your silkiest robe, for the city beckons with its nocturnal allure. Welcome to The Manhattan Diaries—where your nighttime glow rivals the city's most illustrious stars.

BEHIND THE VELVET ROPE

Midnight Facials and East Side Tales

Midnight Facials and East Side Tales unveils the clandestine world of nocturnal beauty in Manhattan, where the city's relentless pace yields to the serene luxury of upscale salons and spas. This chapter delves into more than just skincare rituals; it's an exploration of the intimate moments and whispered stories shared beneath the discreet lighting of the Upper East Side's most exclusive havens of beauty.

> **The Midnight Ritual.** As the city that never sleeps continues its hustle, a different kind of energy comes alive in the salons of the East Side. Here, midnight facials are a ritual, a sacred time for rejuvenation, where the elite come to shed the stresses of their day-to-day lives and immerse themselves in the hands of expert aestheticians.

> **Bespoke Skincare Journeys.** Every facial is a unique journey, tailored to the individual stories of Manhattan's diverse inhabitants. From anti-aging miracles to revitalizing treatments, these sessions are not just about beauty; they're about maintaining a certain standard of living, an unspoken requirement of the city's social elite.

> **Confessions and Camaraderie's.** In the quiet of these late-night appointments, the treatment rooms turn into confessional booths. Between the soothing strokes and nourishing masks, clients share their hopes, dreams, and fears, forging a bond with their beauticians that goes beyond the skin's surface.

> **The Science of Beauty.** These exclusive salons are where science meets luxury. Cutting-edge technologies, innovative treatments, and luxurious ingredients from around the globe converge here, offering the city's discerning clientele the ultimate in skincare.

➢ **The Unspoken Code of Discretion**. In this world, discretion is key. What happens in these midnight sessions is a well-guarded secret, part of the unspoken code of the Upper East Side. It's a realm where privacy is cherished, and trust is paramount.

➢ **The Aromatherapy Experience**. Immerse yourself in the transformative power of aromatherapy during these midnight facials. Custom blends of essential oils are tailored to soothe the mind and enhance the mood, turning each session into a sensory journey that rejuvenates both the skin and the spirit.

➢ **Legacy of Beauty Techniques**. Explore the legacy of ancient beauty techniques that are integrated with modern practices. From Gua Sha and jade rolling to the latest in LED therapy, these techniques are meticulously chosen to uphold the timeless quest for beauty and relaxation among Manhattan's elite.

➢ **Exclusive Membership Perks**. Discover the exclusive memberships that offer more than just skincare. These memberships include priority booking for sessions, invitations to private beauty events, and first access to new treatments, making each client feel like a cherished part of the East Side's select community.

In Midnight Facials and East Side Tales, the allure of Manhattan's nightlife finds its counterpart in the understated elegance of its beauty rituals. These sessions are more than mere appointments; they are a lifestyle, a testament to the city's dedication to beauty, luxury, and the personal stories that weave through its heart. Here, in the sanctuaries of the East Side, beauty is not just skin deep; it's a narrative, rich with whispered secrets and the quiet pulse of a city that always, always, always keeps moving.

Your Triumphs: Midnight Facials Activities

_____
_____
_____
_____
_____
_____
_____
_____
_____
_____
_____
_____
_____
_____
_____
_____
_____
_____
_____
_____
_____
_____
_____
_____
_____
_____

Inspirational Quote

WHATEVER YOU VIVIDLY IMAGINE, ARDENTLY DESIRE, SINCERELY BELIEVE, AND ENTHUSIASTICALLY ACT UPON . . . MUST INEVITABLY COME TO PASS! — Paul J. Meyer

Your Goals: Intentions and Thoughts

The Secretive World of Midnight Beauty

In The Secretive World of Midnight Beauty, we slip into the alluring underbelly of New York's after-hours, where the city's glitz and glamour find refuge in the discreet and luxurious world of late-night beauty rituals. This section isn't just about secret rendezvous for pampering; it's a deep dive into an exclusive enclave where the city's elite engage in the sacred art of preserving beauty and grace against the backdrop of the city's twinkling skyline.

➢ **The Hush of Midnight Appointments**. As Manhattan buzzes with nightlife, a different kind of buzz fills the air in exclusive salons. Here, under the shroud of night, high-profile clients seek refuge for beauty treatments. Midnight is not just an hour; it's a sanctuary of rejuvenation and privacy.

➢ **The Art of Discretion**. In these clandestine beauty sessions, discretion is the unspoken oath. The identity of clients and the nature of their treatments are guarded like precious secrets, a nod to the city's love for privacy and exclusivity.

➢ **Elixirs of Youth and Beauty**. These late-night haunts are where the most advanced, most luxurious treatments are offered. From revolutionary anti-aging therapies to bespoke skincare routines, each treatment is an elixir of youth, tailored to the city's discerning tastes.

➢ **Confessional of the Rich and Famous**. Beyond mere beauty treatments, these sessions are confessional booths for the rich and famous. Between the soothing strokes of facial massages and the delicate touch of beauty tools, whispered confidences are exchanged, making each appointment an intimate affair.

➢ **The Ritual of Preservation**. In this world, beauty treatments are ritualistic. They're about maintaining a standard, upholding an image that aligns with the high stakes of Manhattan's social and professional circles. It's a commitment to oneself, a testament to the power of appearances.

➢ **The Allure of Exclusivity**. These midnight beauty sessions are not just about the treatments but the exclusivity. Access to these after-hours appointments is as coveted as invitations to the city's most exclusive events, with clientele lists more guarded than the guest lists of underground speakeasies.

➢ **Innovative Techniques from Around the Globe**. The treatments offered blend global beauty secrets with modern innovations. From age-old Eastern massage techniques to the latest in French skincare technology, these sessions are a melting pot.

➢ **The Transformation Before Dawn**. As the city sleeps, its most influential faces undergo transformations. These midnight sessions are where tired skin is revitalized, and the stresses of the fast-paced city life are massaged away, ensuring that with the break of dawn, a new, refreshed persona is ready to face the world.

➢ **The Scent of Midnight Luxury**. Beyond skin and facials, the experience is heightened by the luxurious ambiance—the soft lighting, the plush furnishings, and the exclusive scents that fill these spaces, creating an atmosphere of opulence and tranquility.

The Secretive World of Midnight Beauty is an ode to the hidden, nocturnal beauty culture of Manhattan, where the pursuit of aesthetic perfection goes beyond vanity. It's about the allure of the night, the intimate secrets of the city's elite, and the art of maintaining a facade that can withstand the relentless pace of New York life. In these late-night beauty sanctuaries, each treatment is a whisper in the ongoing conversation of elegance and allure, echoing through the streets of a city that, even in its quietest hours, is vibrantly alive.

BEHIND THE VELVET ROPE

Your Triumphs: Late Night Beauty Rite Activities

Inspirational Quote

IF YOU BELIEVE IN YOURSELF AND HAVE DEDICATION AND TENACITY AND NEVER QUIT, YOU'LL BE A WINNER. THE PRICE OF VICTORY IS HIGH BUT SO ARE THE REWARDS. — Bear Bryant

Your Goals: Intentions and Thoughts

Moonlit Elixirs and Rituals of Transformation

Moonlit Elixirs and Rituals of Transformation invites us into the enchanting world of Manhattan's midnight beauty scene, where the city's rhythm slows and a more intimate narrative unfolds. Here, under the soft caress of moonlight, the city's most exclusive salons and spas become stages for transformative rituals, blending ancient beauty secrets with the allure of modern luxury. This section isn't just about skincare; it's a journey into the heart of personal metamorphosis, performed in the city's most secretive hours.

- ➢ **The Charm of Moonlit Treatments**. As the city lights dim, a different kind of illumination begins. In these exclusive enclaves, moonlit treatments offer a unique ambiance, where the tranquility of the night enhances the efficacy of serums and elixirs, making each application a sacred ritual of rejuvenation.

- ➢ **Alchemy of the Night**. The products used are no ordinary concoctions; they are moonlit elixirs, imbued with ingredients that harness the restorative power of the night. From lunar-charged water to nocturnal blooms, these elements are believed to hold the secret to enhanced beauty and vitality.

- ➢ **Whispers of Ancient Wisdom**. Each ritual is a nod to ancient beauty practices, an ode to times when skincare was intertwined with mysticism and moon phases. This blend of old-world wisdom with contemporary science creates a unique experience that speaks to the soul as much as the skin.

- ➢ **The Transformation of Self**. These rituals go beyond the skins' surface, serving as transformative experiences. Amidst the soothing ambiance and gentle touch of skilled aestheticians, clients find themselves on a journey of self-discovery and renewal, emerging not just with radiant skin but with a rejuvenated spirit.

➢ **Exclusive Circles of Beauty**. Participation in these moonlit rituals is akin to entry into an exclusive circle, a coven of beauty where secrets are shared, and bonds are formed. In this space, each individual is part of a select group that understands the true essence of Manhattan's nocturnal beauty.

➢ **The Intimacy of Personalized Care**. In these moonlit sanctuaries, every treatment is deeply personalized. Aestheticians become confidantes, crafting treatments that cater not just to skin types, but to life stories and emotional states, ensuring each ritual is as unique as the individuals who seek them.

➢ **Serenade of the Senses**. These rituals are a serenade of the senses. The soft melodies that float through the air, the luxurious textures of the creams and oils, and the subtle scents of night-blooming flowers—all combine to create an immersive experience that lulls the clients into a state of blissful tranquility.

➢ **The Ephemeral Beauty of Night Ingredients**. Special emphasis is placed on ingredients that bloom and reveal their potency at night—jasmine, evening primrose, and moonflower. These nocturnal wonders are prized for their ability to nourish and rejuvenate, embodying the mysterious power of the night.

Moonlit Elixirs and Rituals of Transformation is more than a chapter about beauty treatments; it's a celebration of the mystical, transformative power of the night in Manhattan's high society. In the quiet hours, away from the public eye, these rituals offer a chance to not just maintain beauty but to rediscover and reinvent oneself. It's in these moonlit moments that the true magic of Manhattan's beauty culture reveals itself—a blend of luxury, tradition, and the transformative power of the night.

Your Triumphs: Rituals of Transformation Activities

_____

_____

_____

_____

_____

_____

_____

_____

_____

_____

_____

_____

_____

_____

_____

_____

_____

_____

_____

_____

_____

_____

_____

_____

_____

_____

_____

_____

_____

_____

Inspirational Quote

GIVE LIGHT, AND THE DARKNESS WILL DISAPPEAR OF ITSELF. — Desiderius Erasmus

MIDNIGHT FACIALS AND EAST SIDE TALES

Your Goals: Intentions and Thoughts

157

The Allure of Ageless Manhattan

The Allure of Ageless Manhattan is a foray into the city's unyielding pursuit of timeless beauty, where the quest for agelessness transcends mere vanity and becomes a symbol of the city's own relentless spirit. In this section, we delve into the heart of New York's obsession with eternal youth, a narrative woven not just in the elite salons and spas but in the very ethos of Manhattan—a city that refuses to grow old.

> ➤ **The City That Never Ages**. Manhattan itself is an emblem of agelessness, with its ever-evolving skyline and undying energy. This spirit is mirrored in its inhabitants, who embrace a lifestyle that defies the passage of time, seeking beauty treatments and wellness rituals that promise to keep them as vibrant and dynamic as the city they call home.

> ➤ **The Sanctuaries of Timelessness**. Explore the exclusive spas and salons that are temples to agelessness, offering everything from revolutionary anti-aging treatments to ancient rejuvenation secrets. These places are not just about erasing lines but about celebrating the ageless spirit, a testament to the city's mantra of living every moment to the fullest.

> ➤ **The Cutting Edge of Anti-Aging**. Dive into the innovations at the forefront of anti-aging, from groundbreaking skincare technology to the latest in cosmetic procedures. In Manhattan, the pursuit of agelessness is backed by science and luxury, a combination that offers the city's elite the most advanced options in their quest for eternal youth.

> ➤ **The Lifestyle of the Ageless**. Beyond skincare, the Manhattan ethos of agelessness permeates every aspect of life—from fitness and nutrition to mindfulness and stress management. It's a holistic

approach, where maintaining a youthful essence is as much about mental and physical health as it is about appearance.

➢ **The Icons of Ageless Beauty**. Celebrate the icons of Manhattan who have become symbols of ageless beauty. These are the trendsetters and trailblazers, the men and women who redefine what it means to age gracefully, exuding elegance and vitality regardless of the years.

➢ **The Role of Art and Culture**. Explore how Manhattan's rich art and culture scene contributes to its ageless allure. Engagements with theater, museums, and classical music not only enrich the mind but also keep the spirit youthful, providing a cultural elixir that rejuvenates from within.

➢ **Community and Social Connections**. Highlight the importance of community and social connections in maintaining an ageless lifestyle. The vibrant social life of Manhattan, from charity galas to exclusive clubs, fosters relationships that support emotional health and well-being, key factors in staying young at heart.

➢ **The Psychology of Agelessness**. Examine the psychological aspects of the pursuit of agelessness in Manhattan. Understanding how maintaining a youthful outlook impacts mental health and overall life satisfaction can provide deeper insights into why the city's residents are so invested in this eternal chase of youth.

The Allure of Ageless Manhattan is more than just a glimpse into the city's beauty culture; it's an ode to a place where age is just a number and youthfulness a state of mind. In this chapter, we uncover how Manhattan's obsession with agelessness is less about the fear of growing old and more about the celebration of an enduring zest for life. It's a narrative that reflects the city itself—constantly renewing, forever young, and eternally alluring.

BEHIND THE VELVET ROPE

Your Triumphs: Timeless Beauty Activities

Inspirational Quote

A CHAMPION IS SOMEONE WHO GETS UP WHEN HE CAN'T. — Jack Dempsey

160

Your Goals: Intentions and Thoughts

Your Goals: Intentions and Thoughts

9

Penthouse Plump and Pluck: Perfecting the Brow Game Overlooking NYC

Manhattan, a city that doesn't just gaze upon its inhabitants—it studies them, with each arch of a brow echoing tales of intrigue, defiance, and an impeccable sense of flair. In this metropolis of grand gestures, it's not just about the statement you make, but the frame in which you present it—with sophistication, artistry, and a dash of drama.

Now imagine: You're sashaying down Madison Avenue, and while many are smitten by your ensemble, it's the perfection of your brows that casts an entrancing spell. Honey, that's the Manhattan Brow Majesty—a mastery so sublime, it accentuates every emotion, every smirk, every side-eye with theatrical precision.

In this beguiling chapter of The Manhattan Diaries, we ascend to the city's most luxurious penthouses, where the elite perfect the fine art of the brow. From the natural feathery touch to the bold statement arch of a diva commanding her domain, you'll learn the nuances of brow artistry that sets one apart in the concrete jungle.

But this isn't merely about aesthetics. It's about capturing the city's essence, about framing your eyes with tales of love, ambition, and the occasional scandal. It's about understanding the allure of the skyline and ensuring your brows echo its timeless grandeur.

Join me, as we navigate the salons of Fifth Avenue, the boutiques of SoHo, and the hidden chambers of Central Park West, refining an artistry that doesn't just elevate your look, but defines the gaze of the city itself. Because, sweetheart, in Manhattan, every arch is a silent soliloquy. Ready for tweezers and palette, for the city beckons with its brow challenge. Welcome to The Manhattan Diaries—where your brows become the skyline that the world admires.

The Essence of Manhattan in Every Arch

In The Essence of Manhattan in Every Arch, we delve into the artful world of eyebrow sculpting, where each carefully crafted arch speaks volumes in the language of New York City's high society. This section isn't just about grooming; it's an exploration of how the city's essence is captured and reflected in the arches that frame the windows to the soul. In Manhattan, where style and subtlety reign supreme, the perfect eyebrow is a silent testament to one's place in this ever-evolving metropolis.

➤ **The Brow as a Metaphor for Manhattan.** In the city that never sleeps, the eyebrows are more than facial features; they are metaphors for the city itself. Bold and defined arches reflect the city's towering skyscrapers and unwavering confidence, while softer, more natural brows mirror the understated elegance of its historic brownstones.

➤ **The Artistry of Brow Shaping.** Here, brow shaping is elevated to an art form, a careful balancing act performed by the city's most skilled aestheticians. Each stroke, each pluck, is a strategic decision, contributing to a look that defines not just a face, but an attitude, a lifestyle.

➤ **Brow Trends Reflecting City Dynamics.** Just as Manhattan is constantly changing, so too are the trends in eyebrow fashion. From the thick, bold brows reminiscent of the city's bold '80s era to the more refined, natural looks of today, the evolution of brow styles in Manhattan mirrors the city's own historical and cultural shifts.

➤ **The Personal Branding of Brows.** In Manhattan, your brows are an integral part of your personal branding. They speak before you do, telling a story of who you are and what you represent. Whether in a boardroom or at a gallery opening, the right brow shape can be a powerful tool in one's personal arsenal.

- ➢ **The Rituals and Routines**. For many in Manhattan, the routine of brow maintenance is a ritual, a moment of self-care amidst the hustle of the city life. It's a time for reflection, for preparation, for facing the city with one's best face forward.

- ➢ **The Influence of Cultural Districts**. Manhattan's diverse cultural districts influence brow styles. The bohemian chic of Greenwich Village may inspire more natural, expressive brows, while the polished sophistication of the Upper East Side often translates into perfectly sculpted arches, showcasing how different neighborhoods leave their mark on beauty standards.

- ➢ **Celebrity and Fashion Impact**. The brows of Manhattan's celebrities and fashion icons often set the trend. From runway models to film stars, these public figures' choices in brow shaping can spark a city-wide trend, demonstrating the interplay between high fashion, celebrity culture, and everyday beauty rituals.

- ➢ **The Psychology of the Brow**. Delve into the psychology behind brow styling in Manhattan. The way one chooses to style their brows can reflect personal attitudes and self-perception, offering insight into their character and how they wish to be perceived in the competitive landscape of the city.

The Essence of Manhattan in Every Arch is more than just a chapter about eyebrow aesthetics; it's a reflection of how the minutiae of personal grooming can encapsulate the spirit of an entire city. In Manhattan, where every detail matters and first impressions are paramount, the perfect arch is not just a statement of beauty, but a symbol of one's place and power in the city's grand narrative. It's where the arch of a brow can tell a story as compelling as the city itself.

Your Triumphs: Brow Arch Activities

Inspirational Quote

YOUR PERSONAL BRAND IS WHAT PEOPLE SAY ABOUT YOU WHEN YOU ARE NOT IN THE ROOM—REMEMBER THAT. AND MORE IMPORTANTLY, LET'S DISCOVER WHY! — Chris Ducker

Your Goals: Intentions and Thoughts

BEHIND THE VELVET ROPE

The Sanctuaries of Brow Artistry

In The Sanctuaries of Brow Artistry, we step into the hallowed halls of Manhattan's most esteemed brow boutiques, where the shaping of an eyebrow transcends mere grooming and becomes an art form. This section is a celebration of the exclusive salons and hidden gems across the city, where the arch of a brow is crafted with the precision and passion of a master artist. In these chic sanctuaries, nestled among the bustling streets and towering skyscrapers, the city's brow artisans work their magic, transforming each client's visage into a masterpiece of expression and style.

> ➤ **The Artisans of Arch**. Meet the revered brow artisans of Manhattan, whose skillful hands have shaped the faces of the city's elite. These are the unsung heroes of beauty, artists who understand that the perfect arch can elevate a face, communicate confidence, and reflect an individuals' essence.

> ➤ **The Ambiance of Elegance**. Step into salons that are oases of elegance and luxury. Each space is designed to soothe and inspire, from the plush velvet chairs to the soft, ambient lighting—creating an atmosphere that's as refined as the services offered.

> ➤ **Customization and Care**. Discover the personalized approach to brow artistry that these salons champion. Here, consultations preceded treatments, ensuring that each brow shape is tailored to complement the client's facial structure, style, and personality—a true bespoke beauty experience.

> ➤ **Innovation Meets Tradition**. In these salons, cutting-edge techniques coexist with time-honored methods. Whether it's threading, waxing, tinting, or the latest in semi-permanent makeup, each method is executed with a blend of innovation and reverence for traditional practices.

> **A Sanctuary for the Senses**. Beyond brow shaping, these spaces offer an escape from the city's relentless pace. They serve as sanctuaries where clients can unwind, indulge in a moment of self-care, and merge not just with impeccable brows but with a renewed feeling of sense.

> **The Legacy of Techniques**. These salons not only offer modern treatments but also embrace the legacy of ancient brow-shaping techniques from around the world. From the precise art of threading derived from South Asian traditions to the delicate touch of tweezing influenced by European practices, these methods are a nod to the global influences that shape Manhattan's beauty scene.

> **Focus on Holistic Beauty**. Many of these brow sanctuaries in Manhattan emphasize a holistic approach to beauty. They integrate skincare treatments and advice into the brow shaping experience, understanding that the health and texture of the skin surrounding the brows are as crucial as the brows themselves.

> **The Social Scene of Brow Grooming**. These sanctuaries often double as social hubs, where Manhattan's elite gather not just for beauty treatments but for the camaraderie and networking opportunities they present. The experience of getting one's brows done is as much about socializing and connecting as it is about aesthetic enhancement.

The Sanctuaries of Brow Artistry paints a vivid picture of the places in Manhattan where beauty is not just achieved but celebrated. In these sanctuaries, each brow is a canvas, and every artisan's touch is a stroke of genius. It's here, among the city's beauty cognoscenti, that the brow is elevated from a mere facial feature to an emblem of individuality and grace—a subtle yet powerful testament to the sophistication and spirit of New York City.

BEHIND THE VELVET ROPE

Your Triumphs: Brow Sculpting Activities

Inspirational Quote

IF YOU DON'T GIVE THE MARKET A STORY TO TALK ABOUT, THEY'LL DEFINE YOUR BRAND'S STORY FOR YOU. — David Brier

Your Goals: Intentions and Thoughts

The Art and Drama of the Brow

The Art and Drama of the Brow turns the spotlight on Manhattan's magnificent obsession with eyebrows, where each arch and curve is not just a feature but a statement, a dramatic expression of self. In this section, we delve into the world where brows are not merely groomed, but crafted and celebrated as integral elements of one's persona. Here, in the heart of New York City, the shaping of a brow is an art form imbued with drama and personality, reflecting the vibrant tableau of the city itself.

➤ **Brows as Expressive Art**. In Manhattan's beauty circles, eyebrows are canvases for expression. Each arch, each line, tells a story—of boldness, subtlety, sophistication, or rebellion. The art lies in sculpting brows that enhance not just facial features, but also mirror an individuals' character and mood.

➤ **The Drama in its Detail**. The drama of the brow lies in its detail. The slightest variation in shape can transform a look, conveying a range of emotions from surprise to serenity. Manhattan's brow artists are masters of this nuance, understanding that in the city's high-stakes social scene, every detail counts.

➤ **Celebrity and Runway Inspirations**. The brow trends gracing the runways and the faces of Manhattan's celebrities often dictate the city's brow aesthetics. These styles trickle down from the catwalks and red carpets to the city streets, where they are embraced, adapted, and reinvented.

➤ **Innovations in Brow Beauty**. Manhattan's status as a beauty capital means it's always at the forefront of innovations in brow grooming—from microblading and lamination to the latest in tinting techniques. These innovations keep the city's brow game not just on-trend but ahead of the curve.

➢ **The Emotional Impact of the Perfect Arch**. Beyond aesthetics, the perfect brow carries an emotional impact. In a city where first impressions can make or break opportunities, a well-defined brow can be a source of confidence and empowerment, a subtle armor in the urban jungle.

➢ **The Influence of Historical Beauty Icons**. Manhattan's brow aesthetics are often inspired by the timeless styles of historical beauty icons. From the classic arches reminiscent of Audrey Hepburn to the bold statements of Frida Kahlo, these iconic looks continue to influence modern brow trends, blending past elegance with contemporary flair.

➢ **The Power of Transformation**. Highlight the transformative power of a well-crafted brow. A change in brow shape can redefine a face, alter perceived expressions, and dramatically shift one's appearance, showcasing the profound impact of this art form.

➢ **Personalized Brow Styling Sessions**. Explore the rise of personalized brow styling sessions, where clients receive one-on-one consultations to determine the best brow shape for their lifestyle, personality, and career. It's a tailored approach that goes beyond standard grooming, offering a customized brow experience.

➢ **Brow Maintenance as a Ritual**. In Manhattan, brow maintenance is more than a routine; it's a ritual. Regular appointments, touch-ups, and at-home care are all part of the city dweller's commitment.

The Art and Drama of the Brow is more than a chapter on eyebrow aesthetics; it's a tribute to the power and poetry of the brow in Manhattan's beauty narrative. Here, each brow is a work of art, a slice of drama, reflecting the city's pulse and the stories of its people. In Manhattan, where life is lived on a grand scale, the art and drama of the brow are not just beauty rituals but essential acts of self-expression, as bold and dynamic as the city itself.

Your Triumphs: Brow Drama Activities

Inspirational Quote

IT'S IMPORTANT TO BUILD A PERSONAL BRAND BECAUSE IT'S THE ONLY THING YOU'RE GOING TO HAVE. YOUR REPUTATION ONLINE, AND IN THE NEW BUSINESS WORLD IS PRETTY MUCH THE GAME, SO YOU'VE GOT TO BE A GOOD PERSON. YOU CAN'T HIDE ANYTHING, AND MORE IMPORTANTLY, YOU'VE GOT TO BE OUT THERE AT SOME LEVEL. — Gary Vaynerchuk

Your Goals: Intentions and Thoughts

Brows as a Symbol of Personal Evolution

In Brows as a Symbol of Personal Evolution, we delve into the intimate narrative of how eyebrows in Manhattan have come to symbolize not just beauty or trend but personal growth and evolution. This section takes us through the transformative journey of brow artistry, where each arch and line mirrors the life changes, milestones, and inner journeys of the city's denizens. Here, in the bustling heart of New York, the evolution of one's brows becomes a poignant testament to their personal story.

> ➤ **The Journey from Youth to Maturity**. Trace the evolution of brow styles from the carefree, perhaps unruly brows of youth to the more defined and sophisticated arches of maturity. This transition often reflects a person's journey from seeking identity to defining it, a parallel to the ever-evolving skyline of Manhattan.

> ➤ **The Bold Statement of Change**. A drastic change in brow shape can often signal a significant life event or personal transformation. Whether it's embracing a natural, fuller brow after years of over-plucking or opting for a daring, sculpted look, each change marks a chapter in an individual's life story.

> ➤ **A Reflection of Self-Discovery**. The way one chooses to style their brows can be a reflection of self-discovery and self-acceptance. It's a celebration of individuality, where each person finds the shape and style that truly expresses who they are or who they aspire to be.

> ➤ **The Influence of Cultural and Social Shifts**. Just as Manhattan responds to cultural and social shifts, so do the trends in brow styling. These shifts often inspire changes in personal style, with brows acting as indicators of one's adaptability and engagement with the world around them.

➢ **A Barometer of Confidence and Power**. The evolution of one's brows can also be a barometer of growing confidence and empowerment. As individuals climb the ladders of their personal and professional lives, their brows often grow bolder, more defined—a silent but powerful expression of their stature and self-assurance.

➢ **The Resurgence of Past Styles**. In Manhattan, the resurgence of past brow styles often mirrors one's nostalgia or homage to a bygone era. From the thin, penciled brows of the roaring '20s to the thick, natural arches of the '70s, these retro revivals can signify a person's connection to certain periods or sentiments in their life.

➢ **Brows as a Canvas for Artistic Expression**. For many, brows become a canvas for artistic expression, experimenting with colors, embellishments, or even temporary tattoos. This bold approach to brow styling can be a form of personal artistry, reflecting one's creative spirit and willingness to defy conventional beauty norms.

➢ **The Influence of Professional Life on Brow Styling**. In a city like Manhattan, where career and image often go hand in hand, changes in brow styles can correlate with professional evolution. From more conservative shapes suited for corporate environments to bold styles embraced by creative industries, brows can reflect one's professional journey and aspirations.

Brows as a Symbol of Personal Evolution is more than a chapter on a beauty trend; it's a story about personal growth and expression set against the dynamic backdrop of Manhattan. In this city, each brow's arch and curve are more than aesthetic choices; they are the silent narrators of personal journeys, evolving and adapting as one navigates through the complexities and triumphs of life. Just as Manhattan continues to reinvent itself, so too do its inhabitants through the artistry of their brows.

Your Triumphs: Personal Evolution Activities

Inspirational Quote

IF THE WORLD SEEMS COLD TO YOU, KINDLE FIRES TO WARM IT. — Lucy Larcom

Your Goals: Intentions and Thoughts

BEHIND THE VELVET ROPE

The Trendsetters and Brow Icons

In The Trendsetters and Brow Icons, we sashay into the world of Manhattan's eyebrow elite, where trendsetters and icons dictate the styles that frame the city's most alluring faces. This section isn't just about following trends; it's about the individuals who set them, the bold and the beautiful who define what it means to have 'the perfect brows' in a city that's always watching. Here, in the glamor-drenched streets of New York, the shaping of a brow is as influential as the latest fashion on Fifth Avenue or the newest show on Broadway.

- ➤ **The Celebrities Setting Brow Trends**. Celebrities in Manhattan often become the unintentional or intentional trendsetters for brow styles. Whether it's a pop star's daring new look or an actress's return to classic elegance, their choices often create ripples across the city, influencing how countless New Yorkers frame their eyes.

- ➤ **Fashion Industry Influencers**. The designers and models dictating New York's fashion scene also play a significant role in setting brow trends. The runways of Manhattan's fashion week can introduce bold new brow concepts, turning avant-garde ideas into mainstream must-haves.

- ➤ **The Social Media Brow Gurus**. In the digital age, social media influencers and beauty bloggers have become pivotal in shaping brow aesthetics. With their tutorials, product recommendations, and personal style choices, they reach a wide audience, turning personal preferences into widespread trends.

- ➤ **Historical Figures as Brow Inspirations**. Manhattan's fascination with brows isn't just contemporary; historical figures and old Hollywood glamour icons continue to inspire. The timeless styles of these past legends offer a nod to classic beauty, reminding us that some trends are truly eternal.

➢ **The Makeup Artists Behind the Scenes**. The unsung heroes of the brow world are the makeup artists working behind the scenes. These professionals, armed with tweezers and palettes, craft the looks that grace magazine covers and red carpets, often igniting the next big trend in brow fashion.

➢ **The Role of Cultural Movements**. Cultural movements and shifts often inspire new brow trends in Manhattan. From the bold statements of the feminist movement to the artistic influences of the city's diverse subcultures, these broader societal changes can be reflected in the way people choose to style their brows.

➢ **The Impact of Theatrical and Cinematic Styles**. The theatrical and cinematic worlds of Manhattan, from Broadway to indie films, often set trends in brow styles, influencing the beauty choices of New Yorkers.

➢ **Beauty Industry Innovators**. The innovators and entrepreneurs in Manhattan's beauty industry also play a crucial role as trendsetters. These individuals, through the introduction of new products and techniques, often dictate the direction of brow aesthetics, from natural enhancements to high-definition styles.

➢ **The Influence of International Styles**. As a global melting pot, Manhattan's brow trends are also influenced by international styles.

The Trendsetters and Brow Icons chapter is a tribute to those who shape Manhattan's brow culture, a culture that is as much about individual expression as it is about collective style. In this city of endless transformation, these trendsetters and icons are not just following fashion; they are fashion, each one contributing to the evolving narrative of beauty and self-expression in the world's most glamorous urban jungle. Their influence goes beyond the arch of a brow; it's a reflection of the city's pulse—ever-changing, always captivating.

Your Triumphs: The Perfect Brows Activities

Inspirational Quote

CHANGE YOUR THOUGHTS AND YOU CHANGE YOUR WORLD. — Norman Vincent Peale.

Your Goals: Intentions and Thoughts

Your Goals: Intentions and Thoughts

10

Harlem to Tribeca: Beauty Blends and Cultural Trends Across the Burroughs

Manhattan, a city that doesn't just hear melodies—it feels them, as each beat reverberates stories of heritage, passion, and vibrant cultural tapestries. And in this symphony of a metropolis, it's not just about moving to the rhythm; it's about creating it—with grace, authenticity, and a mosaic of influences.

Now imagine: You're dancing through Harlem's historic streets, each twist and turn revealing a blend not of the shoes you wear, but the cultural medley you embody. Darling, that's the Manhattan Mélange, a dance of beauty that speaks of history, legacy, and a splash of modern flair.

In this enthralling chapter of The Manhattan Diaries, we'll journey from the soulful corners of Harlem to the contemporary vibes of Tribeca, unearthing the beauty rituals and cultural imprints that paint the city's vast canvas. From the afro-centric hair designs that narrate tales of pride to the avant-garde makeup hues of downtown's elite, you'll discover the beauty blends that make Manhattan a palette of endless inspiration.

But this isn't just about surface allure. It's about diving deep into the city's roots, about wearing beauty that tells a story—a tale of diversity, of evolution, of dreams birthed in the intersections of tradition and tomorrow. It's about cherishing the landmarks and the tales they whisper, creating a look that's quintessentially Manhattan.

Join me, as we stroll the avenues from uptown to downtown, imbibing the essence that doesn't just adorn you, but becomes a living testament to the city's cultural heart. Because, sweetheart, in Manhattan, every beauty ritual is a homage to its rich tapestry. Grab your beauty kit and passport to the past, for the city's chronicles beckon. Welcome to The Manhattan Diaries—where your beauty is as diverse and captivating as the city's own saga.

Harlem's Heritage and Beauty Legacy

Harlem's Heritage and Beauty Legacy opens a window into the soulful heart of Manhattan, where the rich tapestry of African American history has woven an enduring legacy of beauty and style. This section is not just a stroll through a historic neighborhood; it's an exploration into a cultural bastion where beauty rituals and styles resonate with the deep, rhythmic beats of heritage, resilience, and pride. Here, in the vibrant streets of Harlem, every hairstyle, every beauty choice tells a story, echoing the voices and visions of generations.

➤ **The Renaissance of Hair**. Harlem has long been a center for African American hair culture, from the sophisticated styles of the Harlem Renaissance to today's natural hair movement. This neighborhood has pioneered trends that celebrate texture, natural beauty, and self-expression, influencing wider beauty narratives in Manhattan and beyond.

➤ **Icons of Harlem Beauty**. Explore the iconic figures who have shaped Harlem's beauty scene. Legends like Madame C. J. Walker, who revolutionized black hair care, and contemporary influencers who continue to redefine what beauty means, showcasing the neighborhood's ability to blend tradition with innovation.

➤ **The Barbershop and Salon Culture**. Dive into the unique culture of Harlem's barbershops and salons. These places are more than just venues for haircuts and styles; they are community hubs, spaces of belonging and conversation, where the latest trends meet the timeless art of storytelling.

➤ **The Influence of Music and Art on Beauty**. In Harlem, the worlds of music, art, and beauty are inextricably linked. Jazz, hip-hop, and street art have all left their mark on beauty trends, creating styles that are bold, expressive, and unapologetically individualistic.

> **Beauty as a Form of Resistance and Empowerment**. Harlem has long used beauty as a tool for resistance and empowerment. From the afros of the Civil Rights movement to the contemporary embracing of natural textures, hairstyles in Harlem have made powerful statements about identity, equality, and pride.

> **Skincare's Stylish Saga**. Uncover the chic evolution of skincare in Harlem, where timeless traditions meet the buzz of modern innovation. Dive into a world where local botanicals are not just ingredients but stars of a glamorous skincare lineup, influencing today's organic beauty sensations with a touch of Harlem's historical flair.

> **Runway Rendezvous**. Step into Harlem's fashion scene, where every street corner doubles as a runway and every outfit tells a bold story. Explore how Harlem's signature styles—think jazz age glamor and edgy streetwear—have seamlessly integrated with striking beauty trends to craft looks that are as dynamic as they are stylish.

> **Herbal Elegance and Wellness Wisdom**. Savor the sophisticated legacy of herbalism in Harlem, where generations of wisdom brew beneath the surface of modern beauty practices. These aren't just remedies; they are inherited secrets of wellness and beauty, infused with the soul of the community and embraced by those who cherish a holistic approach to living lavishly.

Harlem's Heritage and Beauty Legacy is a celebration of a neighborhood that has not just observed beauty trends but has created them, influenced them, and lived them. In Harlem, beauty is more than aesthetic; it's a powerful expression of culture, history, and identity. It's in these storied streets that beauty transcends the physical, becoming a symbol of a community's soul, resilience, and enduring legacy in the ever-evolving narrative of Manhattan.

Your Triumphs: Heritage and Beauty Activities

Inspirational Quote

YOUR BRAND IS A GATEWAY TO YOUR TRUE WORK. YOU KNOW YOU ARE
HERE TO DO SOMETHING—TO CREATE SOMETHING OR HELP OTHERS IN
SOME WAY. THE QUESTION IS, HOW CAN YOU SET UP YOUR LIFE AND WORK
SO THAT YOU CAN DO IT? THE ANSWER LIES IN YOUR BRAND. WHEN YOU
CREATE A COMPELLING BRAND, YOU ATTRACT PEOPLE WHO WANT THE
PROMISE OF YOUR BRAND—WHICH YOU DELIVER. — David Buck

Your Goals: Intentions and Thoughts

BEHIND THE VELVET ROPE

Tribeca's Trendsetting Avant-Garde

In Tribeca's Trendsetting Avant-Garde, we immerse ourselves in the chic and cutting-edge world of one of Manhattan's most fashionable enclaves. Here, in the cobblestoned streets and loft-style galleries of Tribeca, beauty and style are redefined with each passing season. This chapter is not just about the latest trends; it's a deep dive into a neighborhood where the avant-garde is the norm, and where beauty standards are as dynamic and artful as the district's famed contemporary art scene.

- ➢ **The Intersection of Art and Beauty**. Tribeca, known for its art galleries and film festivals, creates a unique intersection where art directly influences beauty trends. Makeup and hair become extensions of artistic expression, with bold colors, experimental styles, and innovative techniques mirroring the neighborhood's creative pulse.

- ➢ **The Influence of Celebrity and Film**. As home to the famous Tribeca Film Festival, the neighborhood is a hotspot for celebrity-driven beauty trends. The red carpets and premiere events here are often the first places where new, daring looks are debuted, setting the tone for what will dominate beauty counters and salons city-wide.

- ➢ **The Rise of Boutique Beauty Experiences**. In Tribeca, boutique beauty salons and spas offer personalized, unique experiences. These establishments are trendsetters in their own right, often pioneering new services, from bespoke skincare treatments to custom-blended makeup, catering to a clientele that values exclusivity and innovation.

- ➢ **Sustainability and Conscious Beauty**. Echoing the neighborhood's forward-thinking attitude, Tribeca's beauty scene is at the forefront of sustainable and conscious beauty. Organic products, eco-friendly practices, and ethical sourcing are not just preferred but expected, reflecting a deeper awareness and commitment to global and social issues.

➤ **The Digital Influence**. Tribeca's beauty trends are also shaped by the digital age, with influencers, bloggers, and digital content creators playing a significant role. The neighborhood's chic aesthetic is often captured and shared across social media platforms, inspiring beauty enthusiasts far beyond Manhattan's borders.

➤ **The Evolution of Men's Grooming**. Tribeca is also a trendsetter in the world of men's grooming, where traditional barbershops have evolved into luxurious grooming lounges offering a range of services. These spaces cater to the modern man's desire for grooming that goes beyond the basics, encompassing skincare, haircare, and even wellness.

➤ **The Influence of Tribeca's Architectural Aesthetics**. The architectural aesthetics of Tribeca, known for its industrial-chic lofts and historic buildings, also influence its beauty trends. The preference for understated, minimalist makeup and effortlessly chic hairstyles reflects the neighborhood's architectural character and stylish, yet unpretentious, attitude.

Tribeca's Trendsetting Avant-Garde is a testament to the neighborhood's role as a beacon of modern, sophisticated, and socially conscious beauty. In Tribeca, the streets themselves are runways, where the latest trends are not just followed but born, reflecting the neighborhood's standing as a vibrant, influential force in Manhattan's larger beauty narrative. Here, beauty is more than skin deep; it's a reflection of artistic innovation, cultural awareness, and the ever-evolving spirit of one of New York's most dynamic districts.

Your Triumphs: Beauty and Style Activities

Inspirational Quote

YOUR PERSONAL BRAND IS A PROMISE TO YOUR CLIENTS . . . A PROMISE OF QUALITY, CONSISTENCY, COMPETENCY, AND RELIABILITY. — Jason Hartman

Your Goals: Intentions and Thoughts

The Melting Pot of Styles in Midtown

In The Melting Pot of Styles in Midtown, we explore the pulsating heart of Manhattan, where the convergence of cultures, styles, and eras creates a dazzling display of beauty and fashion. This chapter is a vibrant stroll through the streets of Midtown, a place where the latest global trends meet timeless New York chic. Here, the crossroads of the world become the crossroads of style, where every turn reveals a new facet of the city's eclectic and ever-evolving beauty narrative.

- ➤ **Global Influences on the Fashion Runway**. Midtown, with its iconic fashion avenues and flagship stores, is a runway where global influences come to life. From the sleek sophistication of Parisian style to the bold hues of African prints, these influences mingle on the streets, creating a unique blend that's quintessentially Manhattan.

- ➤ **The Business of Beauty in Midtown**. The corporate and business world of Midtown brings its own flavor to beauty trends. Here, the power suit is complemented by power makeup and grooming, where polished, professional looks meet the city's dynamic fashion sense.

- ➤ **The Cultural Tapestry of Street Styles**. The streets of Midtown are a tapestry of diverse cultural styles, reflecting the neighborhood's mix of tourists, locals, and business professionals. Street style photography often captures this eclectic blend, showcasing how global trends are adapted and personalized in Manhattan.

- ➤ **The Influence of Theater and Arts**. Proximity to Broadway and the Theater District means that the dramatic and avant-garde often find their way into Midtown's beauty trends. From theatrical makeup to daring hairstyles, the influence of the arts is unmistakable in this part of the city.

➢ **The Evolution of Classic New York Elegance**. Amidst these diverse influences, Midtown also holds onto the classic New York elegance. The timeless beauty of old Manhattan, with its understated yet sophisticated style, remains a staple, proving that some trends truly are timeless.

➢ **The Impact of International Tourism**. Midtown's status as a tourist mecca brings a constant influx of international styles and trends. Visitors from around the globe leave their mark on the local beauty scene, introducing new ideas and perspectives that blend with Manhattan's aesthetic.

➢ **The Luxury of Fifth Avenue**. The influence of Fifth Avenue's luxury fashion houses shapes Midtown's beauty trends. Here, high-end makeup, skincare, and haircare are not just products but symbols of a lifestyle, reflecting the opulence and prestige associated with one of the world's most famous shopping districts.

➢ **The Accessibility of Diverse Beauty Services**. Midtown is home to a diverse array of beauty services catering to all ethnicities and hair types. From salons specializing in Asian hair techniques to those adept at African and Latin American styles, the availability of such varied services exemplifies the neighborhood's commitment to inclusivity and diversity in beauty.

The Melting Pot of Styles in Midtown is a celebration of Manhattan's unique ability to blend the global and the local, the contemporary and the classic. In this bustling center of the city, beauty and fashion are more than just personal choices; they're a mosaic of the world's cultures, a dynamic dance of styles that exemplifies the essence of New York—diverse, dynamic, and endlessly stylish.

Your Triumphs: Beauty and Fashion Activities

Inspirational Quote

NOTHING IS WORTH MORE THAN THIS DAY. — Johann Wolfgang von Goethe

Your Goals: Intentions and Thoughts

The Evolution of Beauty in the East Village

In The Evolution of Beauty in the East Village, we traverse the eclectic and ever-changing landscape of one of Manhattan's most vibrant neighborhoods. This chapter is a journey through the bohemian and avant-garde streets of the East Village, where beauty has evolved as a reflection of the area's rich artistic and cultural history. Here, beauty trends are not just adopted; they are born from a tapestry of influences, ranging from punk rock edginess to the understated chic of modern bohemia.

> ➤ **From Punk to Modern Boho**. The East Village's history as a punk rock haven in the '70s and '80s has left an indelible mark on its beauty trends. This legacy has evolved into a modern bohemian aesthetic, where edgy, unconventional looks coexist with a more relaxed, natural style.

> ➤ **Artistic Influence on Beauty Trends**. The neighborhood's thriving artistic community continues to influence local beauty trends. Street art, local galleries, and performance spaces inspire bold, colorful, and experimental approaches to makeup and hair, reflecting the area's creative spirit.

> ➤ **The Indie Beauty Scene**. The East Village is a hotspot for indie beauty brands and boutiques. These small, often locally-owned businesses introduce innovative, niche beauty products and services, catering to a clientele that values uniqueness and personal expression.

> ➤ **The Vintage and Thrift Influence**. The prevalence of vintage and thrift stores in the East Village has also impacted local beauty styles. Retro-inspired hairstyles, makeup looks, and a penchant for revisiting past decades' beauty trends are a significant part of the neighborhood's aesthetic.

➤ **Diversity and Inclusivity in Beauty**. Reflecting the diverse population of the East Village, beauty trends here are inclusive, embracing all genders, ethnicities, and styles. This inclusivity is evident in the range of beauty services and products available, catering to a wide spectrum of beauty needs and preferences.

➤ **Impact of Music and Subcultures**. The East Village's rich music scene, spanning punk, indie, and alternative genres, has significantly influenced local beauty trends. The distinct styles of musicians and their subcultures, from the rebellious punk aesthetic to indie artistry, continue to inspire bold and unique beauty expressions in the neighborhood.

➤ **Grassroots Beauty Movements**. The area has been a breeding ground for grassroots beauty movements, championing causes like body positivity, natural beauty, and anti-consumerism. These movements have fostered a beauty culture that values authenticity and self-acceptance, challenging mainstream beauty standards.

➤ **Influence of Local Street Fashion**. Street fashion in the East Village, known for its eclectic and unconventional style, directly influences beauty trends. The fusion of vintage finds with contemporary pieces, often seen on the streets, is mirrored in eclectic and personalized beauty looks that defy categorization.

The Evolution of Beauty in the East Village encapsulates the essence of a neighborhood that has always danced to its own beat. In these streets, beauty is an ever-evolving narrative, a reflection of history, art, and the continuous ebb and flow of cultural trends. The East Village doesn't just follow beauty trends; it sets them, creating a vibrant and inclusive tapestry that mirrors the neighborhood's dynamic, artistic, and unapologetically individualistic spirit.

Your Triumphs: Beauty Trend Influences Activities

Your Goals: Intentions and Thoughts

Your Goals: Intentions and Thoughts

City Roundup:
City Lights and Urban Beauty Chronicles

As we draw the curtain on "Behind the Velvet Rope: NYC's Grooming Secrets Revealed," we find ourselves not just armed with the clandestine beauty secrets of Manhattan, but also with a deeper understanding of how this city shapes it inhabitants—from their outward styles to their inner selves. "City Roundup: City Lights and Urban Beauty Chronicles" isn't merely a conclusion; it's a revelation, a final brushstroke on a canvas that intricately portrays the relationship between this city's soul and the souls of those who walk its streets.

Throughout our journey, we've seen how the artistry in a Tribeca salon, the legacy in a Harlem barbershop, the avant-garde spirit of the East Village, and the cosmopolitan allure of Midtown are not just reflections of personal style but expressions of life stories. Each neighborhood in Manhattan, with its unique beauty rituals and trends, serves as a mirror, reflecting the multifaceted nature of its residents.

We've discovered that in Manhattan, beauty is more than skin deep. It's a dance of identities, a way to express our most authentic selves. From the bold and the beautiful in the high-rises of the Upper East Side to the bohemian chic on the Lower East Side, every style choice tells a story, every grooming ritual reveals a chapter of one's life.

This book, in its exploration of the city's grooming secrets, has peeled back layers, uncovering not just how Manhattanites look, but more importantly, why they look the way they do. It's about the rhythm of the city and how it syncs with the heartbeat of its people. In the boldness of an eyebrow, the elegance of a hairstyle, or the daring hue of a lipstick, there lies a piece of someone's journey, a snippet of their ongoing dialogue with the city that never sleeps.

BEHIND THE VELVET ROPE

As we bid adieu, "City Roundup" leaves us with an appreciation for the beauty rituals of Manhattan as more than just routines; they are acts of self-discovery and expressions of personal narratives. In the end, it's clear: in Manhattan, every grooming choice is a step towards unraveling your inner self, a chance to align with the city's rhythm while dancing to the beat of your own drum. In this city of endless possibilities, your beauty is your story, waiting to be told on the grand, glittering stage that is New York City.

1. Sky-High Lashes and City Lights: Mascara Secrets of the Metropolis

In "Sky-High Lashes and City Lights: Mascara Secrets of the Metropolis," we explore the transformative power of mascara in Manhattan, where eyelashes are not just beauty accessories but storytelling tools that capture the city's essence. This chapter takes you through the elite salons and hidden beauty spots where you'll discover how to prefect your lash artistry, ensuring every blink is as captivating as the city's twinkling skyline. Dive into the Manhattan Diaries, where your gaze commands as much attention as the city lights.

2. The Manhattan Mani-Pedi: Nail the New York Chic, From Tips to Toes

In "The Manhattan Mani-Pedi: Nail the New York Chic, From Tips to Toes," explore the transformative world of nail care in Manhattan, where a mani-pedi extends beyond grooming into a bold personal statement. This chapter of The Manhattan Diaries takes you through elite salons and hidden nail bars, showing how to fashion your nails as a reflection of the city's dynamic spirit—classic, contemporary, and utterly chic. Discover how to perfect your nails not just with color, but with the confidence of Manhattan itself.

3. Central Park Glow: Natural Skin Care in the Urban Jungle

In "Central Park Glow: Natural Skin Care in the Urban Jungle," this chapter of The Manhattan Diaries explores how Central Park inspires natural skincare amidst Manhattan's urban pace. Learn to harness botanicals and minerals that mirror the park's tranquility for a radiant complexion that thrives in the city. Discover skincare that blends the best of nature with New York's dynamic spirit, ensuring your natural glow is as vibrant as the city itself.

4. SoHo Salon Soirees: Hair Dos and Don'ts with NYC's Top Stylists

In "SoHo Salon Soirees: Hair Dos and Don't with NYC's Top Stylists," part of The Manhattan Diaries, we explore the stylish world of SoHo's top hair salons. This chapter reveals how Manhattan's elite stylists shape hairstyles that reflect the city's dynamic blend of glamour and edge. Learn the essential dos and don'ts, and see how each hairstyle narrates its wearer's personal story. Dive into the heart of SoHo where hair is not just styled—it's transformed into a living, telling piece of art.

5. Fifth Avenue Fragrances: Crafting Your Signature Scent Amidst City Scents

In "Fifth Avenue Fragrances: Crafting Your Signature Scent Amidst City Scents," part of The Manhattan Diaries, dive into the art of perfume creation along Manhattan's glamorous Fifth Avenue. Learn how to blend a signature scent that captures your essence and the vibrant spirit of the city. From historic perfumeries to cutting-edge labs, this chapter shows how your personal fragrance can embody elegance, ambition, and the unique mystique of Manhattan, leaving a memorable impression wherever you go.

6. Red Lips and Broadway Hips: Finding the Perfect Shade for Every City Occasion

In "Red Lips and Broadway Hips: Finding the Perfect Shade for Every City Occasion," part of The Manhattan Diaries, we delve into the significance of red lipstick in Manhattan's fast-paced scene. Discover how to choose a red that not only matches the occasion but also captures the city's vibrant spirit and your unique style. This chapter illustrates how the right shade of red can make a powerful statement, turning every smile into a story and every stride into a declaration of confidence. Join us in finding your perfect Manhattan red, where your lips tell tales as compelling as the city itself.

7. Bronzed in Brooklyn: Tanning Secrets for that Year-Round City Sunshine

In "Bronzed in Brooklyn: Tanning Secrets for that Year-Round City Sunshine" from The Manhattan Diaries, we uncover how to achieve the signature Brooklyn Bronze—a glowing tan that captures the essence of Brooklyn's vibrant culture. This chapter takes you through Brooklyn's sunniest locales, offering tips on maintaining a radiant glow that highlights the borough's unique blend of historic charm and contemporary edge. Learn how to shine with the timeless allure of Brooklyn, where every ray of sunshine enhances your natural beauty.

8. Midnight Facials and East Side Tales: Nighttime Rituals of the City's Elites

In "Midnight Facials and East Side Tales: Nighttime Rituals of the City's Elites" from The Manhattan Diaries, dive into the exclusive world of nighttime beauty rituals in Manhattan's elite circles. This chapter reveals the secretive and luxurious treatments that rejuvenate the city's luminaries from dusk till dawn, detailing the transformative facials and serums used behind the Upper East Side's closed doors. Discover how Manhattan's elite align their beauty routines with the city's vibrant energy, maintaining a glow that mirrors the allure of the moonlit metropolis.

9. Penthouse Plump and Pluck: Perfecting the Brow Game Overlooking NYC

In "Penthouse Plump and Pluck: Perfecting the Brow Game Overlooking NYC" from The Manhattan Diaries, delve into Manhattan's high-end eyebrow sculpting scene. This chapter reveals how the city's elite perfect their brows in luxurious penthouses, turning each arch into a statement of style and expression. Learn the art of crafting brows that not only enhance facial features but also reflect the city's architectural grandeur, ensuring every look carries the essence of Manhattan's dramatic skyline.

10. Harlem to Tribeca: Beauty Blends and Cultural Trends Across the Burroughs

In "Harlem to Tribeca: Beauty Blends and Cultural Trends Across the Boroughs" from The Manhattan Diaries, explore how Manhattan's diverse neighborhoods from Harlem to Tribeca shape distinct beauty trends. This chapter delves into the city's cultural mosaic, revealing how traditional and modern style merged to form unique beauty expressions. Learn how each community's heritage influences its beauty rituals, offering a panorama of styles that embody the essence of Manhattan's rich and varied cultural landscape.

Where Do We Go From Here?

As we turn the final pages of "Behind the Velvet Rope: NYC's Grooming Secrets Revealed," we stand at the precipice of a new chapter in The Manhattan Diaries, ready to embark on the next leg of our journey—"Skyline Secrets: How Manhattan's Elite Tame Their Tresses." But before we dive into the luxurious world of Manhattan's most exclusive hair sanctuaries, let's pause and ponder, "Where do we go from here?"

"Where Do We Go from Here?" is not just a question; it's an invitation. An invitation to continue unraveling the layers of our personal style narratives, to delve deeper into the essence of what makes us quintessentially Manhattan, and yet, undeniably unique. In "Behind the Velvet Rope," we uncovered the secrets beneath the surface, the grooming rituals that shape the facades of the city's glitterati. Now, as we transition to "Skyline Secrets," we prepare to ascend to the very crowns of our heads, where the drama and elegance of Manhattan's skyline are echoed in the tresses of its inhabitants.

Imagine each strand of hair as a thread in the vast tapestry of this city. In "Skyline Secrets," we will explore how these threads are woven into statements of power, elegance, and rebellion. We'll uncover the secrets behind the luscious locks that grace the penthouses of the Upper East Side, the edgy cuts that strut through the vibrant streets of SoHo, and the bohemian waves that float effortlessly in the coffee shops of Greenwich Village.

"Where Do We Go from Here?" beckons us to look upwards—to the skyline of this magnificent city and to the crowning glories of its people. It's an exploration of how hair in Manhattan is not just a matter of style, but a symbol of identity, a barometer of the times, and a canvas for personal expression.

So, darling reader, as we bid farewell to the velvet ropes and whispered secrets of grooming, let us step into the light of "Skyline Secrets" with anticipation. The journey through The Manhattan Diaries is far from over. In fact, the most tantalizing secrets are yet to be unfurled, strand by strand, as we continue to unravel the mystique of Manhattan and, in turn, discover the most authentic versions of ourselves.

"Where Do We Go from Here? Is more than a question; it's a promise— a promise of more . . . let the journey continue.

CITY ROUNDUP

Your Triumphs: Recap Activities

_____
_____
_____
_____
_____
_____
_____
_____
_____
_____
_____
_____
_____
_____
_____
_____
_____
_____
_____
_____
_____
_____
_____
_____
_____
_____
_____
_____

Inspirational Quote

TEARS OF JOY ARE LIKE THE SUMMER RAINDROPS PIERCED BY SUNBEAMS.
— Hosea Ballou

Action Items: Intentions and Thoughts

Journal Pages: Pen Your Tales

Journal Pages: Pen Your Tales

Journal Pages: Pen Your Tales

Journal Pages: Pen Your Tales

Journal Pages: Pen Your Tales

Journal Pages: Pen Your Tales

Journal Pages: Pen Your Tales

Journal Pages: Pen Your Tales

Journal Pages: Pen Your Tales

Journal Pages: Pen Your Tales

www.ingramcontent.com/pod-product-compliance
Lightning Source LLC
Chambersburg PA
CBHW032054020426
42335CB00011B/326